MILTON AND AUGUSTINE

Patterns of Augustinian Thought
in *Paradise Lost*

Peter A. Fiore

MILTON
AND
AUGUSTINE

Patterns of Augustinian Thought
in *Paradise Lost*

The Pennsylvania State University Press
University Park and London

Library of Congress Cataloging in Publication Data

Fiore, Peter Amadeus, 1927-
  Milton and Augustine.

  Includes bibliography and index.
  1. Milton, John, 1608-1674. Paradise Lost.
2. Augustinus, Aurelius, Saint, Bp. of Hippo—
Theology. 3. Milton, John, 1608-1674—Religion and
ethics. 4. Fall of man in literature. I. Title.
PR3562.F47   821'.4   80-17854
ISBN 0-271-00269-7

For my sister Mary

Contents

Acknowledgments

Some of my debts are longstanding, long overdue. Three eminent Milton scholars, no longer with us, were a great source of inspiration to me. B. A. Wright gave direction to my path in Milton's theology and curbed many a flight of fancy and imagination; Rosalie Colie, who was a muse to many a colleague, changed my whole attitude toward serious scholarship; Merritt Y. Hughes's wise counsels were a source of encouragement. The late Arthur Brown, my professor at University College, London, was strict and perceptive; his criticisms, always selfless, have been invaluable, as have been suggestions made by Roger Sharrock and F. T. Prince. Lore Metzger, the type of colleague everyone should have, was always ready with insights and mature judgments. Edward Le Comte shared with me his wealth of classical learning and his true understanding of the critical problems posed by Milton's epic. His wife, Mia, beautiful artist that she is, extended hospitality over the years that has been a joy. Louis Andreatta, whose very presence is a cultural influence on anyone who meets him, has seen me through the many months of preparing the manuscript for publication. Kenneth and Elaine Kowald are friends who are ever ready to assist; I know that something of their spirit has entered here.

I have been greatly assisted by the encouragement of John M. Steadman, William B. Hunter, Jr., John T. Shawcross, William Empson, Wayne Shumaker, Giovannina De Blasiis, Kathleen and Jane Lester-Cheney, Albert Labriola, Fred Humphreys, Lawrence Hyman, Lee A. Jacobus, Mario A. Di Cesare, Thomas Kranidas, and all those other fine colleagues in the exciting Milton Seminar. I am especially grateful to Roland Mushat Frye, who read the manuscript and saved me from more than one error of fact and judgment. For all limitations in the book, however, I am solely responsible.

The staff in London's British Museum most graciously provided me with much necessary material and a comfortable setting for research and writing. Some of the material in this book has appeared in one shape or another elsewhere. I am grateful to the editors of *Milton Quarterly, The Huntington Library Quarterly, The CEA Critic,* and the *Milton Encyclopedia* (Bucknell University Press) for allowing me to use and reshape my original material. I am very thankful for Vergene Leverenz, who read the manuscript and offered invaluable suggestions.

Above all, I owe a personal debt of gratitude to my mother who has been "to mee...all things under Heav'n."

CHAPTER 1

Introduction

Although there has seldom been any question in the minds of Milton scholars that the theology of Augustine, "the most judicious of all the Fathers," exercised an influence of some consequence on Milton's thinking, surprisingly, a complete study of this influence on the poet's treatment of the Fall of Man in *Paradise Lost* has never been undertaken. This study attempts such an investigation, concentrating on the three main doctrines inherent in the myth of the Fall: paradisal life (preternatural world), which was lost (Original Sin), and finally recovered (Redemption). Isabel MacCaffrey argues convincingly that the threefold pattern of separation, initiation, and return, following a cyclical or spiral path, characterizes almost all mythical thinking, and Augustine's formula clearly shows the way in which, in the Christian version of the monomyth, all slighter cycles in the history of human endeavor melted into a single gigantic circle comprising the whole of human time.[1] In the Augustinian version of the myth, the brief idyll in the Garden was the first stage in the Christian drama of salvation, the exile of our life occasioned by the Fall was the second, and the recovery of lost paradise was the third. My reading of the poem against the background of this threefold pattern is not intended to locate Milton exclusively as an Augustinian; my aim is to study the poem in relation to the theological tradition that was already fully articulated by Augustine and implicit in Genesis itself. Burton O. Kurth reminds us that to most seventeenth-century readers "it would not have appeared that Milton was breaking entirely new ground, but rather he was bringing the main elements of the Christian tradition into clearer focus within the scope and unity of a full-scale epic design."[2]

Interest in the work of Augustine, aroused during the sixteenth century among humanists, Christian philosophers, Reformers, and theologians of every variety, continued unabated into the following century. As theology was more seriously studied, so the standard of learning and scholarship among

1

thinkers tended to rise, and interest in Augustine proceeded from an enlightened desire to find an authentic and ancient authority for original speculation.[3] Protestants, Catholics, and Puritans alike professed the unique authority occupied by Augustine in the history of Christian thought; the prodigious Milton was not a man to be unaffected by this authority. An extract from his *Commonplace Book* reveals that Milton knew *De Civitate Dei*; more than forty-five references to Augustine in the prose tracts argue for the poet's espousal of the Father's ideas on church discipline and civil government; and Augustine's definition of Original Sin, cited in *Christian Doctrine*, gives evidence of the fact that the poet drew explicitly from the Father for a doctrine that is most central in a treatment of the Fall of Man.

Before he entered school at the age of seven, Milton studied languages under the learned direction of Thomas Young, the renowned patristic scholar, and if, as Arthur Barker tells us, Milton owed much of his patristic learning to Young's direction,[4] then we can be certain that the boy was exposed to the most prolific of all the Church Fathers in the original Latin at a relatively early age. At St. Paul's, which Milton entered about 1620, the old rule of John Colet was still pretty much in force, and this rule insisted that the Fathers of the early Christian era be studied.[5] Joseph H. Lupton, discussing the esteem in which Colet held Augustine, observes that "Colet, as a matter of fact, quotes Augustine oftener than any other Father, nowhere with disapproval, and, more than with the addition 'praeclare dicit'."[6] It is not surprising that Milton, as early as the *Elegia Quarta*, written when he was only eighteen years of age, should inform his readers of the respect he has for the Church Fathers as well as for the Scriptures.

Nor is it surprising that so much pulpit literature of the seventeenth century reveals the esteem preachers had for the authority of Augustine. The years between 1600 and 1675 were heavy in pulpit influences. The Puritan preachers held the ear of England, and their zealous, articulate, and learned sermons directed the lives of many a scholar, poet, and Stuart Englishman. Protestant preachers in general, and Puritans in particular, professed to scorn all authority but the Bible in their teaching, yet relied faithfully on the authority of Augustine when it came to matters of doctrine and dogma. Puritan theology was mainly Calvinistic. Calvin's theology was based on that of earlier Reformers, especially Luther, and his gifts of logic and clear expression made him preeminently the theologian of Protestantism in general. That Augustinian theology was a stimulus in Luther's and Calvin's teaching is even superfluous to explain; that Augustine figured prominently in the homilies of the preachers is evident from even a cursory reading of the sermons. William Haller says that these preachers, "Calvinist though they were in varying degrees, referred as often to St. Augustine as to the author of the Institutes."[7] In doctrinal matters and on issues of controversy, Augustine was invariably the authentic authority cited to buttress a view. For the zealous preachers he was the "great and profound Divine," the "famed father of Puritanism," the "famous Disputer" of "orthodox antiquity," the "noble prelate" whose "sweet councels"[8] in *De Civitate Dei* set the standard for all future preaching.

The lengths to which certain thinkers went in manipulating Augustine's authority for their own purposes can be seen in a work entitled *St. Austin's Religion wherein is manifestly proved out of the Works of that Learned Father, that he dissented from Popery, and agreed with the Religion of the Protestants in all the main Points of Faith and Doctrine—Contrary to the Impudent, Erroneous, and Slanderous Position of the bragging Papists of our Times, who falsely affirme, we had no Religion before the times of Luther and Calvine.* The work was printed in 1624 and was sold at St. Dunstan's churchyard. At the outset, the author states:

> Whereof, to make some shew unto the world, Torrensis a Iesuit in the yeare 1569 published in Latine a Collection, out of St. Austin's workes, as all such speeches as he thought made in any sort for them, and against us; intiteling that his Collection by the name of Confesio Augustiniana; So about two yeares since, one Brereby Priest (whether Secular, or Iesuit, I know not) hath published in English such an other Collection, out of the same St. Austin's workes, intitling it, St. Austin's Religion. Now for the discovery of this their insolent bragging of St. Austin, I have

thought good, to undertake the proving of this asserion.
Viz. That St. Austin was rather of our Religion, then of the
Papists: for as such, as in most materiall points he is
undoubtedly for us, and against them.[9]

And the fight is on, with the author listing sixty-two teachings
of Roman Catholicism and disputing each with tenets of Protestant doctrine, using in each instance innumerable quotations
from the works of Augustine. Although the work does not have
the smooth, argumentative style and tone of many of the literary
exchanges between the Puritans and other factions in the late
sixteenth century and early seventeenth century, it is reminiscent
of the *Admonition Controversy* which marked the beginning of
those ecclesiastical disputes which raged through the latter years
of Elizabeth I's reign. In the *Admonition Controversy*, Thomas
Cartwright and John Whitgift draw exclusively from the authority of Augustine in the exchange. Whitgift cites innumerable
passages where Cartwright has used the authority of Augustine
incorrectly; and, as proof, Whitgift employs entire passages from
Augustine, maintaining that quoting Augustine "maketh (little)
for your purpose, and...aptly serveth mine."[10] Cartwright, in
reply, accuses Whitgift of "open violence doone unto Au-
gust(ine's) wordes"[11] and goes on to cite passages where Whitgift
uses Augustine erroneously. Such recourse to Augustine, so
diversely interpreted, attests to the fact that the Father's teachings were very much in evidence during the period and were
open to learned and scholarly examination; in controversy, the
more the Father is used, the more one scores a point over the
other.

Richard Stock's *A Stock of Divine Knowledge, being a lively
description of the Divine Nature*, published in 1641, is another
document of some significance in evaluating Augustinian influences on the young Milton. The importance of the work lies in
the fact that, like William Ames's *The Marrow of Sacred Divinity*, it is a plainly written exposition of Protestant doctrines
which Milton himself shared in the early 1640s. Stock quotes
from Augustine on nearly every page. He discusses at length
Puritan teaching on the attributes of God, the divine inspiration
of Scripture, the doctrine of grace, and the Trinity, all from the

viewpoint of Augustinian teaching.[12] That Augustine was a favorite of Stock's is evident from his very short eulogy preached in 1614, *The Churches Lamentation for the Losse of the Godly*, wherein he mentions Augustine eight times. Although Stock preached at St. Mildred's in Bread Street, he spent most of his time at the church in Allhallows which stood only a short distance from the Milton home on the other side of the way. He died soon after Milton's departure for Cambridge. Despite the fact that the preacher receives no mention anywhere in Milton's references to his childhood, he must have been, as William Haller assures us, a familiar figure, exercising at least the usual degree of influence which such men bore over such households.[13] From such a Puritan preacher, Milton may have first heard the epic of man's Fall and Redemption from an Augustinian viewpoint. If he did not hear the sermons, he may very likely have read them since most sermons were printed and distributed to parishioners some days after they were preached.

The three main aspects of Protestant and Puritan worship were the primacy of Scripture, the proclamation of the word of God, and conversion through rigorous discipline; and the preachers, regardless of their persuasion, did not hesitate to search the works of Augustine for sermon material. The ultimate principle of Protestantism was the doctrine of the authority of the Bible as the pure word of God. The Puritans were the extreme champions of this doctrine, inasmuch as they rejected the authority of the Church and relied on the inner light of the individual soul in interpreting the Scriptures; they proclaimed the complete and unique authority of the Bible. Every learned preacher was aware of the fact that in *De Civitate Dei*, more widely read in the sixteenth and seventeenth centuries than in our own, Augustine's account of the two cities is based mainly on Scripture, and that he "frequently calls, not upon human wit, but upon God's help to aid him in the writing."[14] Augustine wrote prolifically on the use and interpretation of Scripture, and the preachers quoted faithfully from *Speculum et Liber de divinis scripturis, De Genesi ad Litteram, Lectiones in Heptateuchon, Adnotationum in Job Liber Unus*, and the many other works containing his theory of exegesis of the sacred texts. Richard Sibbes, for example, who regarded Augustine as his favorite patristic writer, employs the Father's exegesis through-out his *Commentary on the First Chapter of the Second Epistle to the Corinthians*, without any qualifications.[15]

But for the Puritans, the Bible was not merely a unique authority for the purposes of exegesis. It was, rather, a complete authority containing the principles of all truth, a directory con-taining detailed regulations for all human concerns. Conse-quently, the preacher's aim was not only to explicate the Scriptural texts from the pulpit, but, even more, to convince the faithful of the importance of reading the Scriptures themselves. Robert Bol-ton, in *Saints sure and perpetuall guide*, says, "Here then Aus-tin: Neither let this be sufficient for you, that in the church you doe heare divine reading; but also in your houses, either doe you your selves read, or get others that can reade, and do you will-ingly hearken."[16] Joseph Hall, who was not a Puritan but was certainly conciliatory toward them, reminds the faithful: "What can be more full and clear than of St. Augustine, In his quae aperte, etc. In these things, which are openly laid forth in Scrip-tures are found all matters that contain either faith, or man-ners."[17] Puritan thought held that, since man's nature had become corrupted, he was utterly incapable of worshipping God aright until God should lighten his darkness and comfort his discomfort. Richard Stock teaches:

> Saint Augustine, having given certain rules, by which a man might understand the Scriptures saith thus, if any man by these rules cannot understand the Scriptures, let him not blame the Scriptures, but let him blame himself: as if one saith me, do shew a star with my finger, and he hath a weak sight and cannot see it, let him not blame my finger, but his own weaknesse: for conclusion, every man ought to get a Bible, what wants man for salvation and spirituall comfort, that is not here? there is no distresse, but here is a remedy for it; no discomfort but here is a comfort.[18]

Believing themselves bound by the word of God, the preachers felt that they were not asserting opinion, or a reasonable convic-tion, but the declared will of God, for "it is manifest by Augus-tine, who plainly teacheth, that only the Scripture cannot err, all other writers may err...."[19] John Hales (not a Puritan), like the

6

many Protestant churchmen, followed the example of Augustine in basing his teaching on the Bible as the word of God:

> Let me request you bear with me, if I be such a one as I have St. Austine for example. For it is not my depth of knowledge, nor knowledge of antiquity, nor sharpnesse of wit, nor authority of councils, nor the name of the Church, can settle the restless conceits that possess the minds of many doubtful Christians: only to ground for faith on the uncontroversable text of Scripture.[20]

The second important principle in Puritan worship was proclaiming the word of God. The importance of preaching consisted in the fact that it was the declaration by the preacher of the revelation of God, confirmed in the hearts of the hearers by the interior testimony of the Holy Spirit. Many believed that in the Puritan order of worship the sermon rightfully usurped the position of the prayers and praises, as well as of the sacraments. Augustine's conversion through the spoken word was an ever-recurring theme in the sermons of the century. In his *Confessions*, Augustine tells us that after St. Monica's arrival in Milan he accompanied her each Sunday to hear the sermons of Ambrose; and these sermons, he assures us, were greatly instrumental in his conversion. That faith comes through hearing was a foregone conclusion for all the major preachers, and most likely the reason for such care and eloquence as was put into the delivery. Richard Sibbes says: "We come as his ambassadors. Therefore, considering whose message we bring, they must take it in good part to be told of their sins in a good manner. As St. Austin saith very well, saith he Christ speaks to the sea and it was quiet. Christ said, 'Be still', the sea heard and the waves were still."[21]

But it was Richard Greenham, the most characteristic of the Puritan itinerant preachers, who best exemplifies for us the "preaching" and "hearing" aspect of Puritan worship. For more than twenty years, Greenham's brilliant sermons drew many hearers and were frequently taken down in church and widely circulated in numerous written copies.[22] For Greenham, the preacher was the man of God, the prophet who declared to the congregation the mystery of the Gospel, unfolding the whole plan of salvation, under compulsion to bring men to the parting of the ways that lead to salvation or damnation. On the effectiveness of proclaiming the word of God, he says: "As Augustine saith, The word is compared to an hammer, to a fire, to a sword, and not for nothing. The hammer bruiseth, so the sword must soften our hard hearts; the fire purgeth and purifieth, so the word purgeth our grosse affections, and purifieth our hearts. ..."[23] Greenham's sermons describe the spiritual complaints, doubts, fears, and despairs that penitents brought him, and the remedies which his knowledge of God's will and the counsels of Paul and Augustine had taught him to apply. In a short work called *Godly Instructions*, he cites Augustine more than twenty-five times as a source of consolation for the needy. He emphasizes the great abyss that separates God from man, making it infinitely important that God should cross it and speak to man through the ear and heart.

> But as there is a speaking to the heart, so there must be a hearing of the heart also, and then we hear with our heart, when we fetch up our heart to our eares, and our sounde pearceth them both: then we hear with the heart, when we hear not only with these hollow gristles, but we hear with the Spirit, and we hear with the understanding also: and then we hear with the heart (saith Augustine) when it is with us and the word.[24]

The arguments employed to win men to a life of virtue were not new with the Puritan preachers. M. M. Knappen maintains that "almost all of them can be found in the writings of that master psychologist, Augustine";[25] the preachers neglected very few of them for their propaganda. Indeed, Greenham utilized all the arguments and devices in pulpit oratory; but it was his smooth delivery, his eloquent "sound," his gift of words, that won the hearts of the hearers.

The final major characteristic of Puritan worship was conversion through rigorous discipline. After having impressed upon the minds of the faithful that God should be worshipped according to the "purity" of the Holy Word, the preacher then insisted that God must be served with a corresponding "purity" of life. Augustine's example of a sinful life, conversion with rigorous discipline, and, finally, tranquillity in the way of the Lord was a favorite of the preachers.[26] Just as Greenham enumerated the doubts and questions of parishioners, many of the Puritan ministers made a specialty of answering particular questions which were put to them on all manner of problems connected with the Christian life. These difficulties were called "cases of conscience," and the cases were often discussed in the light of Augustine's experiences.[27]

The Puritan moral standard was formidable in the extreme. Despite the fact that nearly all the preachers accepted Augustine's optimism that God's mercy outweighs any sin of man, they did, however, emphasize a scrupulously rigid doctrine of fear. "Heare what Augustine saith: Doe this for fear of punishment, if thou canst not as yet obey for the love of justice."[28] Joseph Hall says, "Bitter wholsome is a safe receipt for a Christian, saith St. Austin; and what is more bitter, or more wholsome, than this thought. The way not to feel Hell, is to see it, to feare it."[29] Only the most extreme measures are to be urged to save the soul. Robert Bolton says, "Austin, that famous disputer in his time, councelleth to this purpose in this point.... He which heares, if he be not terrified, if he be not troubled, is not to be comforted. Another heares, is stirr'd, stunn'd, takes on extremely; Cure his contritions, because Hee is cast downe and confounded Himselfe."[30] Nicholas Estwick asks, "Do thou whip thy soule with the lashes of divine sentences to follow after God, as St. Austin did his, when it was backeward and resisted this heavenly work of conversion...."[31] In this life it was impossible to eliminate temptation and the tendency to sin, but it was possible and necessary to eradicate any inclination to enjoy or persist in wrongdoing: "...those ancient sins which did shake his [Austin] coate and whispered in his eares, dost thou leave us now? and must we part forever? let not these bosome sins, I say, detaine thee in the prison of the devil, but shake them off."[32] A man must frequently examine his life and conduct to guard against sinful tendencies. So thoroughgoing was to be this examination that the believer was advised that he must in godly jealousy suspect himself of unknown sins, for "Austin held it wisdome to acknowledge a fault where there is none. The wise man saith, I was afraid being sure of the truth, I dread all my doings: that is the reason of the regenerate man."[33] Moreover, the conscientious man should feel sorrow and repent, not only for his own misconduct but for that of his neighbor: "Augustine saith, if thou dost not helpe his eye, God will plague thine eye and his too.''[34] And true repentance and conversion were never too late. Greenham says: "As for young men's consciences, Augustine compareth them to water in a bason, the water is stirred, and there is no face seen: but so soon as maturitie of yeares comes, then it will stand still, and we shall see our faces, and cry with David and Job Lord wipe away the sinnes of my youth.''[35] Late repentance, however, was not the ideal and was to be looked upon with fear and distrust, for "Augustine saith of a young man that had lived riotously in his youth, afterwards converted: I grant true repentence is never too late but late repentence is seldom true.''[36]

The enormous body of writing and the wide scope of topics covered by Augustine provided the preachers with a good deal of material for issues of lesser significance. Henry Burton's condemnation of simony calls on Augustine's ideas about this ecclesiastical abuse,[37] and Robert Bolton's sermons refer often to Augustine's teaching on eschatology.[38] The perplexing problem of predestination and free will found its way into the sermons of the day, and often it was discussed in the light of Book V of *De Civitate Dei*.[39] In the controversy over the manner of prayer, the Puritans advocated extemporaneous expression as opposed to set forms, and they defended their practice by an appeal to the dictum: "Where God dwells, there is his Temple: Wilt thou pray in the Temple, pray in thyselfe, saith Austin.''[40] The zealot William Prynne, whose *Histrio-Mastix* symbolizes more than any other work the attitude of the more rigid Puritans toward the theater, says, "Saint Augustine likewise stiles these Stage-Playes the Pompes of the Devil ... 'Thou art apprehended thou art detected O Christian (saith he) when thou doest one thing, and professeth another: when thou art faithful in name, faithless in works, not keeping the faith of thy promise: going one while into the Church to pray and while after, running to the Playhouse, to crie out impudently with the Stage Players.'''[41] And, concerning the praise and vainglory of this world, "we must remember, that whatsoever eyther we think, or speak of ourselves, or others of us, onely he, as Austin saith, whom the Lord commandeth, is approved: without, or against whom, he that would be condemned of men, shall not be defended of men, whom God judgeth him; nor delivered by men, when God condemneth him.''[42] And worldly knowledge gained out of curiosity or for the sake of itself was a positive sign that a Puritan's intentions were not being directed to the next world. The faithful must

> avoyd curiosity in the search or determination of immateriall or superfluous truths...There are saith Saint Austin two kinds of persons very commendable in Religion: the former, those who have found the truth; the latter, those who doe studiously inquire for it. It is most true of those truths which are important and essential; but to spend ourselves in the search of those truths which are either unrevealed or unprofitable, it is not other than a labour ill lost.[43]

Even the most cursory survey of Reformed literature will indicate the influence of Augustine on the leading Puritan thinkers of the time. As in any religious movement, the bulk of the material is composed of sermons, popular tracts, and commentaries which were little more than collections of expository lectures delivered on this or that Biblical book. The significant thing is that these champions of the "pure" word, who on principle rejected human authority, used Augustine more than any other writer, save Paul. Although this Puritan literature is plentiful and vigorous, it does not, however, reflect a consistent theological system. Knappen observes that "the intellectual backwardness of the movement" is due to the fact that the output on theological subjects was "occasional and controversial rather than thorough and systematic."[44] The Puritans felt capable of defending themselves intellectually against rival religious sects and factions by falling back on Augustine just for the statement of their case against unbelievers and for a sure buttressing of the foundation of their faith. But they were wary about embracing Augustinianism as a theological system. In using Augustine faithfully for the theory of the "pure" word in Scripture, they depart from the doctrine of the medieval church. In emphasizing the elements of fear and rigidity in Augustine's conversion, they often sacrifice that which makes the whole drama of his conversion so magnificent—the hope and optimism that spring from God's mercy, elements which Milton was later to adopt and develop so thoroughly within the massive structure of his two epics of Paradise.

11

CHAPTER 2

The Angelic Fall

Milton's notion of angelic nature in *Paradise Lost*, so Augustinian in its original conception, is important not as an instance of curious and fascinating speculation but as a metaphysical conception which contributes to the central irony of the whole epic. In its totality, *Paradise Lost* deals with heaven, hell, Eden, Adam and Eve, good angels, bad angels, Christ, and God; and the twentieth century has certainly produced its share of reputable critics who have argued that Milton, in ordering his epic, fused these concepts very often in quite a remarkable and orthodox fashion. Yet still more remarkable is the manner in which the poet employed certain doctrinal subtleties underlying these theological concepts—subtleties which function for the dramatic irony of the poem, and, at the same time, confirm and strengthen the poem's overall argument, the final triumph of good. Terms such as essence, substance, accident, nature, and form— provocative as they may have been and still are—were not completely unfamiliar to the better educated minds of the seventeenth century. Where nature meant, for the eighteenth century, those universal truths interwoven with the whole texture of life, and, for the nineteenth century, that great invisible presence felt when looking at a meadow, the seventeenth century saw nature as a more complicated thing, simply because the seventeenth century, it is agreed, was a complicated age. An age that was aware, to a certain degree, of the rational theology of the Cambridge Platonists, a period which produced the *Religio Medici* as a plea for religion in an age of science, a generation which examined the works of Descartes, Hobbes, and Spinoza in their philosophical quest for truth, was bound to understand and employ nature in a very meaningful and profound way.

In an ontological realm, the terms substance, essence, and nature, closely related as they may seem, are quite distinct and have their own individual significance. Substance, the first of Aristotle's categories, is that which exists per se and denotes that which requires no support, but is, moreover, the necessary support of accidents. Essence denotes the intrinsic constitutive elements by which a thing is what it is and is distinguished from every other thing.[1] Nature signifies that which is primitive and original, that which a thing is at birth, and has as its special significance the "principle of motion and activity."[2] Essence and substance, then, imply a static point of view and refer to the constituents or mode of existence, while nature implies a dynamic point of view and refers to innate tendencies. As essence is that whereby any given thing is that which it is, the ground of its characteristics and principle of its being, so its nature is that whereby it acts as it does, essence being considered as the foundation and principle of its operation. Many of the patrological writers, however, preferred to ignore the Aristotelian distinction between essence and nature.[3] For many, the term nature more commonly designated that which constitutes the very being of something—a concept which, in an Aristotelian sense, would be identified with essence.

Augustine, who resented the indiscriminate use of terms, himself often used essence and nature interchangeably; that is, essence or nature is the thing itself or that which makes a thing precisely what it is and nothing else, and which stands in contradistinction to that which proceeds from the free will. By the seventeenth century, many writers in a characteristically patrological fashion did not differentiate between the two terms, and Milton in *Christian Doctrine* and in *Paradise Lost* was no exception. A study of Milton's *Christian Doctrine* attests to the fact that the poet's angelology and its metaphysical implications are fundamentally Augustinian. The persistent goodness of created nature, which Milton treats in Chapter VII of the treatise, is Augustinian; his rather limited treatment of the possibility of spirit transgression, which comes to life dramatically in Book IV of the epic when Satan addresses the sun, falls into a general Augustinian pattern; the poet's notion of pride and the consequent pain and suffering of the fallen angels results from an understanding of nature in an Augustinian sense; and, when Milton insists upon the paradox of good out of evil as a natural outcome in the epic of salvation, a motif which occurs often in the poem, he employs a view which is traditionally Christian and Augustinian.

13

Concerning the notion of nature, Augustine teaches that God, the one, supreme, immutable nature, is the creator of all natures and that, since nature has God for its creator, all nature is meta-physically good.[4] Even that material which is absolutely form-less and without quality cannot be called evil, for it possesses the capacity for form and is consequently a potential good.[5] Con-cerning metaphysical evil in relationship to nature, Augustine argues that evil is not a nature but is nothing.[6] Evil is present in a nature not as something but as a lack of something which that nature must have. One might say that the presence of evil in a nature is really an absence, a privation of being. Willing evilly is a lapse, a failure to act rather than an act, since action proceeds from being and to be is to be in order. No nature, then, that is positive reality, is evil.

But, although for Augustine all nature is good, all natures are not equally good. The things which God has created are all good, and their goodness lies in their participation in God's goodness, yet not equally so.[7] Some natures are more excellent than others, and yet all, from the highest to the lowest order, are good. All is a scale or hierarchy of natures.[8] After asserting that all nature is good and that without nature evil could not exist, Augustine ventures to apply this to human nature, which he always vigorously maintains is weakened by the fatal flaw. But, regardless of this original taint, human nature is not evil—it is simply vitiated.[9] Evil and vice, he insists, only prove that nature is good; the vices themselves are testimonials to the fact that nature is good, for were it not good, vices could not hurt it.[10] Indeed, evil would never have existed had not good nature, though mutable, brought evil upon itself. And this very sin itself is evidence that its nature was originally good. For, just as blind-ness is a vice of the eye, the very fact indicating that originally the eye was made to see the light, so vices in man indicate that his nature was originally good.[11]

In his conception of created nature, Milton is at one with Augustine. Where Augustine teaches that all created reality is good because God created it so, Milton argues that all existing reality is good because it was made out of the substance of God. One of the poet's fundamental beliefs is that all things belong to God and are a unity in him, and that the matter out of which God created man and the universe cannot be considered "an evil thing, nor to be thought of as worthless: it was good, and it contained the seeds of all subsequent good."[12] Nature, which Milton defines in Augustinian terms as "the specific character of a thing, or that general law in accordance with which everything comes into existence and behaves,"[13] is a particular form of matter; and, if matter is good, so too is nature good and incorruptible since it proceeded from God and is part of his eternity.[14] The poet brings the corollary to its fullest expression when he discusses evil in relation to nature. Like Augustine, Milton feels that evil has not a nature, and if it does not have a nature, it must be nothing. Augustine argues that God is the creator of all entity, and it is impossible for the creator of all being to be at the same time the cause of their non-being—that is, of their falling from existence.[15] Milton's doctrine is identical when he teaches that "nothing is neither good nor any kind of thing at all. All entity is good: nonentity, not good. It is not consistent, then, with the goodness and wisdom of God, to make out of entity, which is good, something which is not good, or nothing."[16]

This belief in the persistent goodness of created nature is the basis for Milton's fundamental optimism, his trust in the basic goodness of humanity, and his faith in the final redemption of the world. Moreover, it accounts for those many passages in *Paradise Lost*, so often the cause of disquiet amongst critics, where the excellence of Satan's nature is insisted upon. Satan and the fallen angels have "come from God in an incorruptible state," and their "form and nature . . . ever since the fall" remains incorruptible.[17] So, to conclude from those passages alluding to Satan's "dark'n'd" appearance, "Glory obscur'd," and the host of fallen with "Thir Glory wither'd" (I.612), that their natures are now evil is to conclude that they have lost their existence. It is not surprising then that, standing like a tower, Satan's "form had not yet lost / All her Original brightness" (I.591-92), and still appears as "Glory obscur'd" (I.594). It is with a good deal of metaphysical insight that Milton describes the mighty host of fallen angels "In horrible destruction laid thus low, / As far as Gods and Heav'nly Essences / Can perish" (I.137-39). "Can perish" is an interesting and important stipulation here, for Milton believes that these essences are destroyed only insofar as it is possible for them to be destroyed. Their natures, in virtue of the fact that they exist, are entities; and if they are entities, they are good.

15

This, of course, is not to assert that Satan and the fallen angels are morally good. It simply means that, in an ontological realm, that which exists is good and that which has fallen from existence is evil. Nonentities are not good; and if these fallen angels are now evil, they are nonentities and do not exist. To conclude that Satan's nature is now evil is not only to misinterpret a very important aspect of Milton's metaphysics but, worse still, to deny the existence of Satan's angelic nature as a very important entity in *Paradise Lost*.

Upon this conception that nature retains its original goodness at all costs, Augustine constructs a whole theory on the possibility of spirit transgression which Milton, in creating his Satan, found invaluable for his dramatic purpose. Augustine teaches that a spirit has no ignorance, has no weakness of mind; his nature is so perfect that there is nothing for which he can wish or to which he can aspire. Though he is finite, he is complete in his sphere; and because of his perfection, it is impossible for him to transgress in that sphere.[18] Therefore, the only possible explanation for the fall of the spirits must be that they transgressed in another sphere. If a spirit is taken, so to speak, out of his natural order and placed in another, higher order—the supernatural order—there is the possibility of refusal. The spirit may refuse to accept or to hold something that is above his order; he may, in fact, rebel against that order.[19] The natural goodness of the angel is a singular perfection which is without rival, but to choose supernatural greatness would have been far superior.[20]

Augustine maintains that the angels, from their creation, did not have true and complete beatitude;[21] so their trial must have been one whereby they had a choice to acquire it. Obviously they chose their own natural glory, in its isolation, rather than the community of the supernatural glory; and this is the fall of the angels.[22] That the Incarnation was revealed to the spirits and their unwillingness to adore the God-man was their fall, an aspect which Milton obviously preferred for his dramatic purpose, is merely another expression of the same doctrine.[23] The angels fell through a deliberate opposition to the supernatural, the Incarnation being the highest phase of the supernatural realm and one of which Lucifer and his followers would have no part.[24] Consequently, the repudiation of the Incarnation on the part of Lucifer and his followers was actually a desire for their own natures in preference to a higher perfection. This doctrinal paradox underlies much of the narrative of *Paradise Lost*, and an understanding of Milton's metaphysical thinking provides the reader with a better grasp of the dimensions of the paradox and a better appreciation of the manner in which the paradox functions for the meaning of the poem.

God had created the angelic nature as the most excellent of the created natures; and in Book V of the epic we are told that Satan was the greatest "in Power, / In favor and preëminence" (660–61), while the other angels had the most "excellent intelligence." God loved the angelic nature so much that he created it superior to that of the parents of mankind, who were "Favor'd of Heav'n so highly" (I.30). Beelzebub, describing the progenitors, says: "Created like to us, though less / In power and excellence" (II.349–50). As early as Book II, the reader is introduced to Milton's hierarchical conception, which has the angels in the highest realm of creation and man in the lesser realm of power and excellence. But the angels did not sin because their natures had gone bad. On the contrary, they sinned because they preferred to contemplate too much the magnificence of their own natures, which, in this sense, is rebellion against a hierarchical creation. When Satan rejected God's pronouncement in Book V that the Son would assume first place in the heavenly hierarchy, he actually rejected a whole hierarchical creation which God had formed good but had distributed in various and diverse degrees. Yet in Book I, when Satan assumes first place in the infernal hierarchy, he actually establishes in hell a scale or hierarchy of things which is to prevail until the end of time, and the whole satanic situation results in irony.

The angelic nature, being the most excellent of created natures, is the closest to the image of God—consequently, the most attractive to the angelic will and most easily substituted for God. Satan laments, "Lifted up so high / I sdein'd subjection, and thought one step higher / Would set me highest" (IV.49–51). And the one step was Lucifer's tragedy. God, in his generosity, created Lucifer's nature so close to the image of the Deity that Lucifer became over-enamored with the gift, to the neglect of the giver. Satan is very much aware that the rejection of the community of supernatural glory was not only his downfall but also very much undue his creator, who had destined him one of the highest in the scale of creation: "Nor was his service hard. / What could be less than to afford him praise, / The easiest recompense, and pay him thanks, / How due!" (IV.45-48). In bemoaning the inordinate preference for his own excellence, Satan regrets that his nature had been created the highest in the angelic hierarchy. If he had been created an inferior nature, he would have been created with a lesser degree of causality: "O had his powerful Destiny ordain'd / Me some inferior Angel, I had stood / Then happy" (IV.58-60). In an angelic world, the higher one ascends, the clearer becomes the image of God; and the angels had the clearer image, while Satan as Lucifer had the clearest. God is the free creator who creates gratuitously, and the being most like Him—those most obviously dependent upon God—will have the highest degree of causality and, in that sense, of independence. The danger of falling will be greatest where it is least justified, where the power and goodness of God is most manifest. Adam and Eve, with all their supernatural and preternatural prerogatives, had a lesser degree of causality because they were the lesser in the scheme of creation. As unjustifiable as was the Fall of Man, still more unjustifiable was the Fall of Angels. This, of course, accounts for God's pronouncement, in Book III, that there will be no redemption for the fallen angel as there will be for fallen man (128-34).

Milton's concept of evil is a further development of the Augustinian paradox that the angels fell because of a preference for their own natures. For Augustine and Milton, evil is the perversion of a good nature by a will gone bad; and this opposition of nature and will is the source of their suffering. Satan himself gives a clear explanation of the concept of evil in one of his early speeches to his fellow demons. He says that, if God in "his Providence" seeks to "bring forth good" out of all their plans, then their labor must be to "pervert that end," which is good, and use the good as a "means of evil" (I.162-65). Bad things are good things perverted, and this perversion arises when a conscious creature becomes more interested in himself than in God and wishes to exist on his own. This, of course, is pride, "when the soul abandons him to whom it ought to cleave as its end, and becomes a kind of end to itself."[25] Augustine says that Satan and the fallen angels delighted more in their own power,[26] while in the epic Milton says that Satan "set himself in Glory above his

Peers, / He trusted to have equall'd the most High" (I.39–40). Augustine feels that Satan's prime concern was his dignity;[27] Milton's Satan revolted because he "thought himself impair'd" (V.665). Augustine says that they were enamored rather of their own power;[28] Milton's Satan argues that he is "self-begot, self-rais'd / By our own quick'ning power" (V.860-61). Augustine, in speaking of Satan, uses the expressions "pomp of empire" and "king of Babylon";[29] Milton calls Satan "Emperor with pomp Supreme" (II.510), "great Sultan" (I.348), "Tyrant" (IV.394), and "Monarch" (II.467).

For both Augustine and Milton, the perverted will of the fallen angels is the problem, not an evil nature. It is impossible for a nature to be contrary to God, but not so a will. It is for this reason that Milton insists so strongly on the freedom of the will: "Sufficient to have stood, though free to fall. / Such I created all th' Ethereal Powers / And Spirits, both them who stood and them who fail'd; / Freely they stood who stood, and fell who fell" (III.99-102). And it is Satan's will, which so freely directs itself, in opposition to its nature, which was created good and remains good, that causes him such misery. He says, "Nay curs'd be thou; since against his thy will / Chose freely what it now so justly rues. / Me miserable!" (IV.71-73). In strict adherence to this notion of nature in opposition to the will, Milton constructs an intellectual or inner hell for his Satan contrary to Dante's, where specialized punishments are inflicted for specialized crimes. Whichever way he goes, Satan carries this inner hell with him: "Which way I fly is Hell; myself am Hell" (IV.75). Satan's cries are not of physical pain but of the misery of inner torment: "Under what torments inwardly I groan" (IV.88), and the sight of any good only intensifies his anguish:

> the more I see
> Pleasures about me, so much more I feel
> Torment within me, as from the hateful siege
> Of contraries; all good to me becomes
> Bane.
>
> (IX.119-23)

Throughout the later books of *Paradise Lost*, we follow Satan through a process of spiritual frustration and mental torment, a torment which he assures us is far more intolerable than any suffering that one would find in Dante's hell: "And in the lowest deep a lower deep / Still threat'ning to devour me opens wide, / To which the Hell I suffer seems a Heav'n" (IV.76-78). The source of the angelic evil then, which on the surface is a rebellion against due authority, is actually a will freely misdirected— an outrageous use (abuse) of nature, not an evil nature. Augustine says that the highest good of intelligent beings is to adhere freely to God in love, and to love in other creatures the intentions of God in them. The good angels were those who persisted in God, their common good.[30] Raphael says, "Freely we serve, / Because we freely love, as in our will / To love or not; in this we stand or fall" (V.538-40). The fallen angels, on the other hand, are those who delighted more in their own power, as though it were from themselves:[31] "Such a foe / Is rising, who intends to erect his Throne / Equal to ours...hath in his thought to try / In battle, what our Power is, or our right" (V.724-28). This pretense of deity, this preference for their own power, is actually the source of the angelic suffering; and the whole situation acts as somewhat of a paradox. The more Satan rejects the order of things by asserting his own angelic nature, the more he accomplishes his own unfulfillment; the more the demons attempt to reascend, the more they achieve their own self-damnation. This repudiation of the created order of things in order to assert autonomy, which Satan knows to be one big lie (IV. 42-45), is "the hateful siege of contraries" which plagues him and his followers in the latter books of the epic. In cursing the love of God, Satan curses himself; in freeing himself from God, he enslaves himself; and the whole picture of Satan becomes situation irony.

Augustine's paradox of good from evil is a familiar feature in Milton's epic. The motif is used twice in the seventh book. It is included in the hymn which is sung before the Son journeys out into chaos, and it is part of the celebrations which take place on his triumphant return. However, in the light of the *felix culpa*— a key Augustinian doctrine upon which all of Milton's plan of salvation rests—the paradox of good from evil necessarily becomes the underlying theme which penetrates the whole epic. Milton maintains that "even in sin, then, we see God's providence at work."[32] God, who is infinitely good, "cannot be the source of wickedness or of the evil of crime: on the contrary, he created good out of man's wickedness."[33] And in the epic we are told, "To him / Glory and praise, whose wisdom had ordain'd / Good out of evil to create" (VII.186-88). Vices themselves are testimonials to the fact that nature is good. Evil would not have existed had not nature, good though mutable, brought evil upon itself; and it is out of this evil that God in turn brings forth a greater good.

Milton, convinced of the persistent goodness of created nature, sees Satan's nature continuing to praise God by virtue of what it is. This praise is the "good out of evil" in spite of Satan's rebellion. In this sense, Milton, like Augustine, sees love and praise of God—on quite a different level, however—persisting even in hell. Where God's justice is most manifest, there we find his highest praise. No matter what Satan says or does, he fulfills God's providence. Satan, who himself is hell, praises God when he first sees Adam and Eve: "So lively shines / In them Divine resemblance, and such grace / The hand that form'd them on thir shape hath pour'd" (IV.363-65). Milton maintains that "God gives a good outcome to every evil deed, contrary to the intentions of the sinner, and overcomes evil with good."[34] All of Satan's "malice serv'd but to bring forth / Infinite goodness, grace and mercy..." (I.217-18). In Book III, God sees Satan coming to pervert man—"By some false guile pervert" (93)—and he certainly does; but, "contrary to the intentions," the result is the *felix culpa*, and Satan's "spite still serves / His Glory to augment" (II.385-86). The angels point out

> Who seeks
> To lessen thee, against his purpose serves
> To manifest the more thy might: his evil
> Thou usest, and from thence creat'st more good.
> (VII.613-16)

And Adam is astonished to find that, having been an instrument in Satan's rebellion, he has actually become an instrument for God's providence (XII.469-78).

It is basic to Milton's epic, and to Christianity in general, that the created order is good; and any repudiation of this order only brings forth, in the long run, a further good. Satan's preference for the good of his own nature is a rejection of the hierarchical order of things.³⁵ It is an arbitrary substitution of a potential impossible to realize, and this evokes an immortal frustration and ever present "torment within me" (IX.121). It seems significant that the great leader whose declaration was "Evil be thou my Good" (IV.110) should now admit "thereby worse to me redound" (IX.128–29). His self-assertion amounts to self-rejection,³⁶ and this conflict is explicitly and repeatedly underscored in *Paradise Lost*, so that it becomes a major theme of the epic. The irony of Satan's situation is part of the Christian paradox that the corruption of the best becomes the worst, and from the worst God brings forth the best, and this functions significantly for the central irony of the whole epic. In conforming to the Augustinian tradition on angelic nature, and all the doctrinal subtleties therein, Milton has given to his epic of lost paradise a richer and deeper meaning; and he has strengthened still further his overall argument, the final triumph of good.

CHAPTER 3

Preternatural Life

The question of motivation in the Fall of Adam and Eve has for some years fascinated serious critics and ordinary readers alike: critics, because the portrayal of Adam and Eve appears to have some embarrassing contradictions in the light of a state of perfection; and ordinary readers, because the scenes of Adam and Eve before the Fall, their edenic life-style, their ideal companionship, their connubial bliss, are so fascinatingly beautiful. One evening in England, a Miltonist remarked to me that no film director could ever capture Adam and Eve so beautifully as did Milton in Book IV, when we first encounter them (albeit through Satan's eyes) walking through the garden. In fact, she went on to say, the whole of Book IV is like a masterful film unreeling itself. Indeed the scene is visually beautiful, and, although Milton created his Adam and Eve like a true artist, more important for the purpose of this study is the fact that he handled his patristic and Biblical materials like a careful theologian.

As Adam and Eve appear, we see them as intelligent, relaxed with none of the anxieties that reveal marriage problems, nude without any of the embarrassments that reveal a sense of shame, physically perfect, and in the prime of their lives. For this portrayal, Milton had a good deal of source material from which to draw, particularly Augustine's lengthy and detailed treatment of the proprieties of the first parents in their state of original justice. The Augustinian tradition taught that the progenitors of the human race were endowed with the gifts of immortality, impassibility, superior knowledge, integrity, and divine grace, since they were created in the image of God. All these gifts, save divine grace, are considered preternatural, which term implies that, although these qualities did not belong to Adam and Eve by virtue of their human nature and were no part of that bodily equipment necessary to their being and life as persons, they were bestowed upon them of God's sheer benevolence, as something over and above their purely human faculties and capacities.

These gifts did not put them, as grace did, into a different and altogether higher order of existence; they gave Adam and Eve additional and greater perfection, but they did not raise them above the purely human level. Therefore, Milton's portrayal of the couple as genuinely human is quite in keeping with the Augustinian concept of preternatural existence.

Through the gift of immortality, Adam and Eve were created such that they could live on forever; and this is explicit from the Scriptural text in Genesis ii.16–17, and iii.19. If Adam and Eve had not sinned, they would have not died; they did sin, however, bringing upon themselves and the whole world the penalty of death. We are introduced to this concept in the opening lines of the epic: "Of Man's First Disobedience, and the Fruit / Of that Forbidden Tree, whose mortal taste / Brought Death into the World" (I.1–3). Augustine is quite explicit in maintaining that the immortality of the soul was not lost by the transgression.[1] This was an immortality of the body, which was a prerogative peculiar to the state of innocence. Milton, despite his Mortalism theory which he applies to post-lapsarian man, feels that, prior to the entrance of sin into the world, all parts of man alike were immortal.[2] The first parents were immune from death, not by their nature, but simply by a special privilege.

Augustine insists that it is one thing *not to be able to die*, as is the case with the angels whom God created; and it is another thing *to be able not to die*, which was the way that Adam and Eve were immortal. Adam was immortal not because he could not die (*non posse mori*) but simply because it was not necessary that he should die (*posse non mori*), and the condition was contingent upon strict observance of the prohibition. Probably the major difficulty in understanding this gift arises from the fact that Adam and Eve did not lose their immortality at the moment of transgression. Even Adam and Eve are amazed that they go on living after the transgression. But it must be remembered that it is God's plan that all mankind be saved, not damned; and Milton, in the epic, is trying to justify this. It is not outside the realm of God's omnipotence to put a condition on any gift. Indeed, the whole state of innocence rests on the condition that Adam and Eve observe the prohibition; and the condition of gradually losing their immortality provides Adam and Eve enough time to convert and regain, in a modified fashion, a new kind of paradise—a paradise within which they are "happier far" (XII.587).

Closely related to the gift of immortality is the gift that rendered Adam and Eve freedom from pain and suffering (sometimes called impassibility by traditional theologians). This is deduced from Genesis iii.16: "I will greatly multiply thy sorrow and thy conception; in sorrow thou shalt bring forth children"; and is stated explicitly in the epic—"Thy sorrow I will greatly multiply / By thy Conception; Children thou shalt bring / In sorrow forth" (X.193-95). But we see this gift at work in all those scenes of Adam and Eve before the Fall where we see their gracious demeanor, their perfect bodies, their joy and happiness in each other's presence, their freedom from anxieties and nervous tensions, their blissful existence free from the cares and woes of the world. Yet Augustine's treatment of this gift, free from the exaggerations of other Church Fathers and later commentators on the Scriptures, nicely paves the way for Milton's handling of Adam and Eve exempt from pain and suffering. Augustine says that Adam and Eve lived without any want (*sine ulla egestate*). They had food (*cibus*) and drink (*potus*). There was in their body no corruption (*nihil corruptionis*), nor seed of corruption which could produce in them an unpleasant sensation (*ullas molestias ullis ejus sensibus ingerebat*). They feared no inward disease (*nullus intrinsecus morbus*), no outward accident (*nullus ictus metuebatur extrinsecus*). They had the soundest health (*summa in carne sanitas*), and were exempt from fear of disease (*cupiditate vel timore*) and from all sadness (*nihil omnino triste*).[3] In other words, by virtue of this gift, Adam and Eve were secured from all those pains and evils which are, directly or indirectly, the consequence of sin.

But this does not mean that they were so shielded by this gift that they were wholly incapable of feeling pain. As a matter of fact, Augustine is careful to add that Adam and Eve would have known hunger and thirst because their bodies—which were animal, not spiritual—required meat and drink to satisfy hunger and thirst.[4] To suggest that Milton's dinner scene with the angelic guest is a breach of the preternatural concept of freedom from pain and suffering is to misunderstand what precisely is involved in this privilege. This gift simply implies that Adam and Eve were undisturbed by all those things from which they were protected by virtue of the preternatural gifts. The gift of integrity effectively prevented the principal source of mental sorrow and temptation, which is concupiscence. The immortality of the body necessarily excluded all those sufferings and infirmities which are the forerunners of death. The pains of childbirth and hard labor result from man's mortality; but before sin, in a state of immortality, Adam and Eve were protected from these disturbances.

Adam and Eve's knowledge, which has perplexed Milton apologists, is given limited treatment by Augustine. It is commonly held that Adam and Eve were endowed with knowledge infused by God and not acquired by the exercise of human faculties. In the writings of the early patristics, we find a great deal of exaggeration concerning Adam's intellectual powers. There was a tendency to attribute to Adam knowledge quite close to that which is God's. Scripture gives no explicit information on this point, and Augustine's teaching is mostly deductive and hypothetical—information derived from an understanding of the other gifts. There is no question that Adam and Eve knew the distinction between good and evil; unless they had known it was sinful to disobey the command of God, there would be nothing wrong with their disobedience. They were plainly warned of the unhappy consequences of the transgression; but before sin, they did not know them by experience. Since Adam and Eve were created in adult life, God would have given them that knowledge which was necessary to that state, a knowledge that human beings normally have to acquire through the years of childhood and adolescence.

Augustine maintains that God, at the moment of creation, infused into Adam's and Eve's minds the knowledge which, though they had no choice of acquiring it themselves, was necessary to enable them to lead a properly ordered human life. Doubtlessly, God endowed them with excellent mental faculties and powers of observation by which they would be able to equip themselves quickly with all necessary and convenient knowledge. Augustine says, "He [Adam] set names upon all types of living souls and this was proof of the most excelling knowledge even in the world's letters and laws. For Pythagoras himself is said to have stated that he was the wisest of all men who first set words to things."[5] But this infused knowledge would not include a knowledge of the nature of the supernatural, an understanding of the solar system, or any other highly specialized information that was not necessary for him to lead a properly ordered human life.

In the epic, there is no problem concerning Adam's knowledge of the supernatural. He did not request of Raphael information on the nature of God or the Beatific Vision, although his request for information on the sex life of angels borders on such knowledge; significantly, Raphael cut him short in this discourse, since it was not necessary to his state. But Adam's interest lay more in the natural sphere: the Creation and the Copernican and Ptolemaic solar systems. Unlike Adam's knowledge of words immediately after his creation (VIII.271-73) and his knowledge of the names of the beasts of the earth and the fowls of the air (VIII.349-54), which he got through infused knowledge, the information on the creation and the solar system was not infused. There is no reason to believe that he was out of order to request it or that he was not able to acquire it. In virtue of the fact that the Creator would not abandon man created in adulthood to complete ignorance in matters of religion and morality, that Adam had no parents or teachers to give him the necessary instruction, and that as head of the human race Adam was destined to be its natural guide and teacher, it seems justifiable that he would be given infused knowledge. But to grant him infused knowledge is not to say that his knowledge was substantially different from ours (and how many of us know much about the Copernican and Ptolemaic solar systems). On the contrary, Adam had in the domain of nature a perfect infused knowledge only with regard to such things as were indispensable to enable him and his descendants to live in conformity with the laws of reason. This does not mean that he was not compelled to learn and inquire, or that he was unable to progress in matters of science and culture.

Significantly, then, to Adam's request for knowledge, "the Godlike Angel answer'd mild" (VII.110). Raphael consents to recount "what thou canst attain, which best may serve / To glorify the Maker, and infer / Thee also happier" (VII.115-17). And if Raphael assures Adam that man could have risen gradu-ally on the Scale of Being from one kind of perfection to another kind (VII.155-61), then it is not too rash to conclude that his knowledge, too, could increase and expand coordinately. As Irene Samuel contends, "Through Books V–VIII it becomes increasingly clear that this happy pair are not forbidden to think, to raise questions, to have impulses and notions, to correct false impressions, to deal with their world out of their own developing natures and knowledge. This Eden can contain whatever stuff of life may enable man to become more 'self-knowing, and from thence / Magnanimous to correspond with Heav'n.'"[6] There is no reason whatever for assuming that Adam, because he had the preternatural gift of knowledge, should have been already acquainted with the Copernican and Ptolemaic solar systems. A knowledge of such scientific and specialized matters as these is hardly a necessary prerequisite to leading a properly ordered human life. The scene is not a breach of the preternatural concept.

Augustine's candid treatment of the gift of integrity, which prompted Saurat to protest that the Father is very crude,[7] is a very detailed and thorough examination of preternatural sensuality and provides the basis for Christian teaching on sex in the state of innocence. The gift of integrity consists in the total absence of concupiscence; and concupiscence here, when applied theologically, takes upon itself a much wider application than the limited meaning of fleshly desire. It indicates any and every motion or impulse of the lower faculties or appetites of man's nature that is not under the perfect rule of the higher faculties, the reason and will.[8] All the faculties of man are from God and by their nature tend to find satisfaction in their appropriate acts, which is good.[9] Above all man's sensitive faculties stand his reason and will, which should govern and direct all his actions if he is to live rightly and worthily as a man.[10] Every impulse of man's lower nature not in accord with the dictates of his reason and will is a manifestation of concupiscence. Adam and Eve, before their Fall, did not experience concupiscence; they were gifted with integrity.[11] This is simply and delicately expressed in Genesis. Eve, fresh from God's creating hand, is presented to Adam, "and they were both naked and not ashamed" (ii.25). Adam and Eve felt no undue, disordered impulse to the strongest of sensitive appetites; their reason and will held complete and easy rule over the appetites that are natural to man. Once they fell, however, they experienced the sense of shame caused by the unruly urge of passion, and they covered themselves with fig leaves.

Augustine here is very cautious not to fall into the errors of other Church Fathers in their teaching on the gift of integrity. Augustine insists that this gift did not deny Adam and Eve all the pleasures of the sensitive life.[12] Indeed, later theologians went so far as to maintain that Adam and Eve enjoyed these pleasures of sense even more than post-lapsarian man, since their natural faculties were purer and therefore keener.[13] But the problem of how man in Paradise was able to keep his passions under the absolute control of his reason and will is not an easy one to solve, even for Augustine. He seems to feel that the variety of psychological factors involved, and the wide scope which must be assigned to the will, seem to postulate a rather complicated endowment which enriched the various higher and lower faculties of the soul with habits and enabled these habits to cooperate harmoniously.[14] To simplify the problem by assuming that Divine Providence exercised a special governance by carefully removing all occasions apt to provoke an outbreak of man's animal passions, and in case of actual danger simply withholding the necessary concursus, is to exaggerate the gift of integrity and, furthermore, to deduce that the Fall of the first parents would appear inexplicable or impossible. If you concede this, then you must concede that God could have stepped in to prevent Eve from extending her hand to the apple.

But the question whether, by virtue of the gift of natural integrity, Adam and Eve were able to commit venial sins—infractions of much lighter consequence—was answered by Duns Scotus. Scotus and his followers thought that Adam and Eve must have been liable to err in nonessentials, seeing that they were able to go astray in matters of decisive moment. This line of reasoning is sensible and extremely important in understanding Adam and Eve in the epic; it is one that Augustine gave serious consideration to some centuries earlier, and which I will discuss later in this chapter. But the principle that Augustine insists upon repeatedly is that the whole of Adam and Eve's sensitive life and activity was in complete subjection to the rule of their reason and will. Concerning conjugal union in the state of innocence, most of the patristic writers felt that the act did not take place. Nowhere does Augustine say that Adam and Eve consummated their marriage union before their transgression; he does assert, however, that they would have had conjugal relations without concupiscence had they not transgressed. He says, "It is quite clear that they were created male and female, with bodies of different sexes, for the purpose of begetting offspring, to increase and multiply and replenish the earth, and to deny this is a great absurdity."[15]

He discusses at great length the beauty of sex and the married state and maintains that, just as the other of man's members obediently served the will, so also Adam's and Eve's organs of generation would have been used for the begetting of offspring under the complete control of their wills. But with the Fall, all this control is gone. The shame and covering of the sex organs by Adam and Eve is very significant for Augustine; he sees in this behavior that man's disobedience to himself is what he merits for his disobedience to God. The body is by nature subject to the mind, but, by the inversion of the hierarchy, it becomes the master of the mind. Augustine further asserts that, before the transgression, it is not that there was no movement of the sexual members; it is that there was no movement without the will's consent. But after the transgression, there is an embarrassing example of involuntary bodily movement, and that is why Adam and Eve cover their sex organs. Since the first disobedience, the motion sometimes importunes the will in spite of itself; and other times the motion fails when there is the desire to feel it, so that, though lust rages in the mind, it does not stir the body.[16] In this failure of response, whether positive or negative, in this insubordination of the body to the mind, Augustine sees the marks of disobedience. And further, he insists that, because this insubordination of the body did not exist before the Fall, we cannot presume that marriage and sexual reproduction, then, are the consequences of sin. Marriage was instituted by God in Paradise, and Adam and Eve were to be one, even in a physical sense.[17] The procreation of children belongs to the glory of marriage and not the punishment of sin, and he who feels that there would be no copulation or procreation but for sin makes sin the origin of the holy number of saints and men.[18] Bodily fecundity, subject to the reason and the will, had its role in the first Paradise; and Aquinas was later to presume that its pleasure was greater in Paradise, owing to the greater fineness of the human body before sin.[19]

The gift of integrity accounts, more than any other gift, for the personality of Adam and Eve in the early books of *Paradise Lost*. They are pictured as calm, controlled individuals without any cause to exercise restraint. As long as they observe the command, they are immune from the tensions of concupiscence. Conforming to the Genesis narrative, Milton regards their nakedness without embarrassment as evidence of freedom from disorder in their generative faculties. John Carey sees the word "mysterious" in the line "nor those mysterious parts were then conceal'd" (IV.312) as a source of embarrassment for Milton, thereby ignoring, in this instance, the seventeenth-century meaning of "holy" and "sanctified," as Donne used it in "The Canonization" and as Carey himself understands it in another context in his comment on Adam's reproving of Raphael in the lines "Though higher of the genial Bed by far, / And with mysterious reverence I deem" (VIII.598-99).[20] When Raphael comes to visit them, Eve ("no veil / Shee needed") waits on him without the slightest trace of embarrassment since, "Virtue-proof, no thought infirm / Alter'd her cheek" (V.383-85). The whole visit reflects the even temper of their lives.

Milton repudiates the ancient tradition that Adam and Eve did not have carnal relations before the Fall by putting in the lovely nuptial bower scene; and only by suggestion does he get involved with the problem of possible offspring before the Fall. The reference to the help in the garden as an eventuality does argue for the fact that children would come in the unfallen state. It also bolsters the degree of their adherence to God's command that they increase and multiply the earth. As Eve upon her creation is led to Adam by God, she is aware of her "marriage Rites" (VIII.487); and Adam accommodates her with no hesitation (VIII.507-11). Milton, as if to prepare the reader for the marital scene in Book VIII, inaugurates his famous love passage with the phrase that all was "Innocence and Virgin Modesty" (501). The manifestation of their mutual love and the practice of their marriage rites was to be "not obvious, not obtrusive, but retir'd" (504).

The whole scene argues for reason and the will in complete control of the passions. It has none of the "her hand he seiz'd" (1037) and "led her nothing loath" (1039) of Book IX, where their union has become impetuous and lustful. Adam's gently leading Eve to the nuptial bower here foreshadows the "hand in hand" with which they quit Eden, repentant and fortified with the promise. Merritt Y. Hughes sees "she what was Honour knew" (508) as an allusion to Hebrews xiii.4, "Marriage is honourable in all," which proves that marriage had its honorable place in Eden and was hardly a consequence of sin. Eve "with obsequious Majesty" (509) approved Adam's pleaded reason; and "obsequious," signifying a devoted and gracious demeanor, characterizes the whole scene.[21] In virtue of the dominant effect of purity and innocence which Milton consistently insists upon, Eve's "blushing like the Morn" (511) can hardly be interpreted as an instance of embarrassment. "Blushing," seen in the context of the whole passage, can mean at most a shyness that often is a natural reaction on first meeting someone, especially on the part of someone who had never seen another creature in the whole of her short existence. Dennis H. Burden convincingly observes that the blush "is 'proper' because it springs out of that 'proprietie' of relationship which belongs to true love."[22] It is not too much to presume that Milton used "blush" to strengthen the simile of the line, that Eve shone like the morn or was bright like the morn, rather than to convey the idea that she blushed from a sense of shame for what was to follow.

When Adam confesses "here passion first I felt, / Commotion strange" (530-31), he is not necessarily confessing that his passions have dominated his reason and will during the act. What he is confessing, however, is that this particular marital pleasure is the one he enjoys the most, "in all enjoyments else / Superior and unmov'd" (531-32)—obviously because of the greater fineness of his human body—and which, if left unchecked and allowed to get out of hand, could become a danger. Indeed the whole scene, with its beauty and grace, does suggest more sumptuousness rather than the spiritual detachment we associate with integrity; but when we consider the poetry of the scene, the pastoral images of sight and smell, and the classical references with their exotic implications employed in describing the garden, the marriage bower, the wedding night—which are far more fleshly than spiritual—then the natural impression for the reader is one of sensuousness. And when we consider that Adam's faculties in an unfallen state were purer, keener, and far more refined than those of fallen man, then it is natural for Adam to experience sensitive pleasure far more intensely. Also, the closely related gift of freedom from pain allowed him, moreover, an enormous capacity for pleasure.[23]

But Adam has not violated his preternatural state, because Raphael exhorts: "In loving thou dost well, in passion not" (588); Raphael would not warn Adam of what might happen if it had already happened. It is indeed remarkable how the poet handled this gift in *Paradise Lost*. The two scenes of lovemaking function nicely for dramatic contrast, as has been observed by Rajan and other critics; but, even more, they bring home the Augustinian concept that disobedience to oneself is what one merits for disobedience to God. Adam's impetuosity in the second love scene, weighed against the control of the first, is a dramatic acting-out of an Augustinian concept; and, despite some dodgy moments with sensuality, the whole business is quite theologically correct.

The most important gift given to Adam and Eve was divine grace. This gift was unique because, unlike any of the others, it placed them in a special relationship with God.[24] It completely transcended Adam and Eve's nature, it exceeded the demands and powers of their given nature, and it was one that was completely undue their created state.[25] The gift elevated Adam and Eve to a higher and nobler dignity; it placed them in a real relationship with God, and gave them the pledge of eternal happiness. In a number of the works of Augustine, the word "justice" is used to signify all the gifts given to Adam and Eve; yet, in those works where the Father is discussing grace as a unique gift, we find him equating justice with the theological concept of divine grace. Most commentators on Augustine's works agree, however, that grace is practically synonymous with justice. Since the Genesis narrative indicates that Adam and Eve were created in the image and likeness of God, this interior life is a sharing in God's nature and image. Adam and Eve, then, because of divine grace inherent in their souls, are a reflection of the divine image.

To grasp Milton's concept of grace will always be difficult, because the poet used the term in so many different ways. There is no question that the poet saw grace and creation in the image of God as one and the same thing, yet quite different from the "Prevenient Grace" of Book XI.3. But, because Milton gives so many different meanings to the term "grace" in *Paradise Lost*, and because he does not in *Christian Doctrine* develop the notion with any authority (which is not to imply that he did not have a teaching on grace; he simply did not present it in a systematized fashion as he did his other dogmatic concepts), one must conclude that the poet, for his dramatic purpose, was content to use grace in some general way, devoid of any of its theological connotations. Most frequently, the word is used to mean forgiveness or favor. However, when he uses "divine image" in reference to Adam and Eve, he comes very close to the Augustinian concept. In Book VII (627), the angels rejoice that man is created in God's image; in Book IV (291-92), we are told that Adam and Eve are created in their Maker's divine image and Satan himself sees in them the "Divine resemblance" (363). In all these passages, the image makes them one with God; and this oneness is not only inward, but outward as well: "Abundantly his gifts hath also pour'd / Inward and outward both, his image fair" (VIII.220-21). This particular treatment of grace and divine image as an outward as well as inward resemblance to God is very much in keeping with the poet's teaching on Creation, where everything is derived from the substance of the divinity.

Probably Milton's closest statement to the traditional Augustinian concept of grace is found in *Christian Doctrine*, when he speaks of the second degree of death, which is called Spiritual Death. By Spiritual Death is meant "the loss of that divine grace, and innate righteousness, by which, in the beginning, man lived with God."[26] Here Milton, in calling loss of grace "spiritual death," is implying that grace is a superior kind of life, a habitual state or quality which Augustine taught. Unquestionably, Milton saw grace as a sharing in the divine image; but the many connotative meanings he gives the term, and the fact that the doctrine is never really delineated, must lead us to conclude that the poet had a very eclectic concept of this gift.

The preternatural concepts, as we have seen, allowed Milton a good deal of material from which to draw for his creation of Adam and Eve as very natural and human people. The gifts, which were over and above purely human faculties, were not a constitutive part of man's human nature, and despite the fact that they gave him additional and greater perfection, they did not elevate him, as grace did, to a different and altogether higher order of existence. It is a mistake to see these gifts as making

Adam and Eve totally and completely different from man as we know him today. The gifts were gratuitous and over and above the state of man; when they were withdrawn, Adam and Eve fell back into their natural and human state. But when they had the gifts, they were still human.

Given the gift of immortality, Adam and Eve were immune from dying simply by a privilege, not by their created nature. Immortality was a free gift, but a gift not natural to them. Death was Adam and Eve's natural lot, and after the transgression, they were placed back into their natural condition. The gift that rendered them immune from suffering does not imply that Adam and Eve were wholly incapable of feeling pain. It simply means that they were secured from all those pains and evils which are the consequence of sin, ignorance, and folly. The gift of knowledge pertained to such things as were indispensable to Adam and Eve to live in conformity with the laws of reason. The gift did not, however, embrace all those matters outside this realm, such as science and culture, so they were able, indeed obligated, to inquire and progress in learning. And the gift of integrity did not render Adam and Eve immune to the pleasures of the senses. On the contrary, their enjoyment of pleasures of the senses was far greater than that ever to be experienced by their progeny. The gift of integrity means simply that their whole sensitive life was in complete subjection to the rule of their reason. In the light of this Augustinian teaching, then, Adam's request for knowledge and his confession of the pleasures of sex can be seen in better perspective.

Two other instances in the preternatural garden which have received quite a bit of critical comment are Eve's dream and Eve's pool scene. Concerning Eve's dream, Grant McColley interprets the incident as a fusion of two traditional beliefs: one, that Adam fell on the first day of his creation; the other, that he fell on the eighth day.[27] William B. Hunter sees it as a fusion of the patristic tradition which taught that the devil had great power over dreams and the Renaissance tradition which taught that dreams very often reveal externally an internal disorder.[28] E. M. W. Tillyard, in line with A. J. A. Waldock's theory that Milton actually places the Fall much earlier in the epic rather than in Book IX, states that the poet "anticipates the Fall by attributing to Eve and Adam feelings which though nominally felt in the state of innocence are actually not compatible with it."[29] He feels that no human being can conceive evil entering a mind quite alien to it, and that the mere fact of entrance implies "some pre-existing sympathy." He concludes that the dream has really touched Eve; and "if the dream has disturbed Eve so much, she has really passed from a state of innocence to one of sin."[30]

The observation that evil entering a mind "implies some pre-existing sympathy" is contrary to Milton's ideology and to the Christian and Augustinian tradition, as well. Eve's dream, no matter how evil and disturbing its content, was, after all, a dream providing providential warning to her, and dreams are far from culpable. Eve's immediate disapproval of the dream should convince us that the whole situation was an exercise of the fancy uninfluenced by judgment and consent.[31] Evil may enter the mind in the form of temptation, and the fact of entrance does not imply "some pre-existing sympathy." Augustine teaches that temptation arises from two sources: from the propensity to evil inherent in one as a result of Original Sin; or from the Devil, who can furnish the imagination with his sinful subject matter and excite the lower powers of the soul.[32] Milton's conception of Eve's dream as coming from Satan, aside from its dramatic purpose, has a good deal of orthodoxy about it because Eve has not yet experienced evil; it came from Satan, who, as John S. Diekhoff says, is the one who has already fallen.[33] No matter how vivid and unholy the image may be, no matter how strong the inclination to transgress the law, no matter how vehement the sensation of unlawful satisfaction—as long as there is no consent of the will, there is no sin.

The deliberation of the will as constituting the very essence of sin is the principle that characterizes Augustine's moral theology and occurs repeatedly in the works of Milton. In *Comus* we read, "Virtue may be assail'd but never hurt, / Surpris'd by unjust force but not enthrall'd" (589–90). And later, "Fool, do not boast, / Thou canst not touch the freedom of my mind / With all thy charms" (662–64); and in *Areopagitica*, "the knowledge cannot defile...if the will and conscience be not defil'd" (Hughes, p. 727). In the epic, Milton has Eve disapproving of the dream from the moment she awakens: "O how glad I wak'd / To find this but a dream!" (V.92–93). And Adam consoles the troubled Eve with, "Evil into the mind of God or Man / May come and go, so unapprov'd, and leave / No spot or blame behind." He advises further, "That what in sleep thou didst abhor to dream, / Waking thou never wilt consent to do" (V.117–21), which certainly indicates that she has not yet consented. After the account of the dream comes the morning hymn, which "pray'd they innocent" (209); and, finally, God sends Raphael to caution Adam on how to preserve "his happy state" (234), which, of course, he has not yet lost. Sin begins only at the instant the will approves the idea of sinning, and not at the moment the idea of sinning is conceived.

Eve's glance into the pool immediately after her creation has likewise generated a good deal of critical comment. For Millicent Bell, Eve's gazing into the mirror of the pool reveals to us that she is no longer wholly innocent, that she is already a woman of the world.[34] But there is no reason to infer that Eve gave full deliberation or displayed an inordinate sense of vanity here. It must be remembered that Eve has just been created; she is less than a few hours old; she has never seen her own image or anyone else's. And, as Arnold Stein observes, what can be more perfectly natural and innocent than a "beautiful woman opening her eyes to look into the mirror that happens to be there?"[35] There is more a childlike curiosity than a sense of vanity here; and Wayne Shumaker observes that, even if Eve was tempted for a moment, she decided almost at once that "beauty is excell'd by manly grace / And wisdom" (IV.490–91).[36]

In a preternatural state, this incident is at most the enjoyment of an object presented by the sense of sight, or the experiencing of some new exhilarating knowledge. This dawning of self-discovery, which occupies not more than thirty lines in the text, carries no more stigma than the dream which was "unapprov'd." In a post-lapsarian period, gazing into a mirror can imply sinful pleasure, depending on the inordinate implications; but in a pre-lapsarian world, it is at most, like Adam's conversation with Raphael, the thrill of experiencing something new. If Eve had defied the "Voice" that called her away from the pool, or if she had returned to the pool repeatedly for the purpose of admiring her image, then a very solid objection could be raised on the basis that she was inordinately attracted to the image which she knew from previous visits and experience. But

Milton has placed the incident too close to her creation. He has treated it almost like child's play, which confirms all the more Eve's innocence: "I started back, / It started back, but pleas'd I soon return'd, / Pleas'd it return'd" (IV.462-64). And immediately following the scene, it is the "bliss on bliss," the total simplicity and innocence behind Adam's pressing Eve's lips "With kisses pure," that intensifies the spying Satan's torment. The deliberation which sin requires is lacking throughout. To assert that the Fall, which involved all mankind, began with this glance is untenable. "Sin," says Milton, "is not a predicament to be measur'd and modify'd, but is alwaies an excesse ... and is as boundless as that vacuity beyond the world."[37]

The incidents of frailty prior to Book IX of *Paradise Lost* prompted Millicent Bell to conclude that there had never been a preternatural state, and, as a matter of fact, that there had never been a Fall of Man. So provocative was her study that Wayne Shumaker attacked Bell's theory and defended Milton's doctrine of the Fall of Man along with the fullness of a state of innocence. Shumaker's analysis is so exhaustive that any observation here would be redundant. But much of the difficulty, it seems to me, stems from a failure to understand the Augustinian thought underlying much of Milton's treatment of Adam and Eve in their unfallen world. Bell maintains that the "mind cannot accept the fact that perfection was capable of corruption without denying the absoluteness of perfection."[38] If Adam and Eve were created perfect, then one of the primary qualities of that perfection is freedom; for to be created specially endowed with all the gifts in their highest degree but lacking freedom, even the freedom to fall, is really to be created in a state short of perfection. Arthur Sewell's difficulty seems much the same as Bell's when he says, "If Adam was created so that evil couldn't abide in him, how could he be 'fondly overcome by female charm'?"[39] Sewell, too, sees Adam and Eve's liability (the possibility of sin) as a defect in their perfection, while in reality the absence of this liability would be a defect in their perfection. God created them so perfect that they were free to fall, and to be created in such a free and liable state in no way denies the absoluteness of perfection but confirms it. Bell feels that "there is nothing in the Paradisal state that can furnish cause for Man's lapse from perfection."[40] If this is so, then why was a command given? Choice to do or not to do is implicit in every command. Why did God give them a choice to do or not to do, when, according to Bell, the paradisal state furnished them nothing for the exercise of that choice?

The whole problem stems from the failure to reconcile freedom with perfection, a problem that has perplexed theologians down through the ages and has intrigued enquirers since the time of Milton. Edwin Greenlaw felt that the soul is made up of a rational and an irrational part, and that Adam surrendered to "that irrational principle of the soul which operates through lust."[41] Denis Saurat carried this further by observing that the sexual inclination through which the race is perpetuated and life is transmitted is "the most capable of obliterating reason completely and leading man to the worst folly. And in such obliteration is the abstract typical trait of the Fall."[42] But it is of no use to make Adam's sin consist in any act involving concupiscence, for this vulnerability had no place in him. Moreover, Saurat continues, the Fall of the Angels paralleled the Fall of Man, and "Satan fell through pride. But during the first night of rebellion, sensuality was born in him and his fall consummated in incest."[43] Again, placing of concupiscence prior to the sin of Adam is in opposition to the concept of integrity, one of Adam and Eve's endowments. An effect cannot precede its cause, and concupiscence came about only with the loss of integrity. Saurat, who cites innumerable parallels between Augustine and Milton, fails to recognize one tenet that both thinkers insist upon: that man's lower faculties were in complete harmony with the will and reason.

The problem might be solved, however, by going back further to a basic fundamental concept, a concept or principle which Milton obviously never questioned in *Paradise Lost*—the intrinsic possibility of sin: "I made him just and right, / Sufficient to have stood, though free to fall" (III.98-99), and again, "For so / I form'd them free, and free they must remain, / Till they enthrall themselves" (III.123-25). The intrinsic possibility of sin is a necessary accompaniment to the possession of free will, and both are necessarily included in a state of perfection. The conversation between God and Christ in Book III (80-135) is actually a discourse on perfection, freedom, and the possibility of sin. Then, also, Adam was in a state of probation, and a state of probation implies that one is subject to a test. Adam's test was one of fidelity to and love for the Creator: "Not free, what proof could they have giv'n sincere / Of true allegiance, constant Faith or Love" (III.103–4). Adam had no equal on earth, none even to come near him in power and honor and endowments, because God made him that way: "He had of mee / All he could have" (III.97–98). The Creator had made all living things subject to him. God had made him lord of all. But he was not God. God was above him; and Adam, with the view before him of all this good given him, freely made his choice.

In the fourteenth book of *De Civitate Dei*, Augustine, along with treating the intrinsic possibility of sin, teaches in essence that in Adam's sin an evil will preceded an evil act. It is a teaching that goes back to the time of St. Paul, and one which Milton used quite logically for his dramatic purpose. There is no question that a sequence of events constituted Eve's fall. Like most departures from perfection, no one makes a momentous decision to choose the way to evil. It is a gradual slipping into sin. This gradual slipping into sin characterizes a will which is giving way to pride; it is a weakening of the will which precedes the fatal act, but it is not the fatal act. Augustine insists in Chapter XI of the same book that the first evil will, which preceded all men's evil acts, was rather a kind of falling away from the work of God, "defectus potius fuit quidem ab opere Dei...."[44] In *De Corruptione et Gratia*, where he discusses this problem in far more detail, Augustine anticipates the many difficulties of some Milton enquirers.

The question has been placed to Augustine in respect to the possibility of Adam's fall from perfection. He answers,

> He did not have perseverance because he did not persevere in the good in virtue of which he was without defect. The fact is that at a certain time a defect appeared in him; and, if so, before this happened he was without defect. It is one thing not to have any defect; but another thing not to continue in that goodness wherein there was no defect. We do not say that he was never without defect, but that he did not continue without defect; and thereby we clearly show that he once was without defect, and that his guilt lies in not having continued in that state of goodness.[45]

40

Consequently, that Adam had no perseverance stems from the fact that he did not persevere in that goodness in which he was without sin. He began to have sin from the point at which he fell (*coepit enim habere vitium ex quo cecidit*), and if he began, certainly he was without sin before he began (*et si coepit ante-quam coepisset, utique sine vitio fuit*). It is one thing not to have sin, and it is another thing not to abide in that goodness in which there is no sin. There is a remarkable consistency between this teaching of Augustine and Milton's treatment of Adam and Eve before the Fall. The incidents prior to Book IX which have led critics astray simply indicate that Milton is getting down to basic Christian concepts—that before the act of disobedience, there was a weakening of the will, a slipping or falling from perseverance, a failing to abide in that goodness in which there is no sin. And the actual fall into sin took place with the eating of the apple. Milton's God did not say "Thou shalt not look into mirrors," or "Thou shalt not talk of things that influence your dreams," or "Thou shalt not ask too many questions about the solar systems or the sex life of angels." He said, in speaking of the Tree of Knowledge, "Remember what I warn thee, shun to taste, / And shun the bitter consequence" (VIII.327-28). Doubtlessly, the incidents of frailty prior to the Fall were instrumental toward the fatal step. It would have been better if Adam had been less curious about the forbidden tree and had talked less about it to Eve, so as not to influence her dreams, or if he had heeded his own advice when he hopelessly discouraged her from going out alone: "Seek not temptation then, which to avoid / Were better" (IX.364-65); because these imperfections, which weaken the will toward approval, can be ruinous, which certainly was the case. But, at most, they are imperfections. In a post-lapsarian world, curiosity, inquisitiveness, and vanity are the effects of sin. In a pre-lapsarian world, they are manifestations of frailty which indicate that the progenitors of the human race failed to persevere in that goodness where there was no sin.

CHAPTER 4

Original Sin

The two doctrines most central to the theological framework of *Paradise Lost* are Original Sin and Redemption. They are mentioned in the opening lines of the epic, "Of Man's First Disobedience" and "till one greater Man / Restore us," and they are strong and persistent, without any theological theorizing, throughout the poem. Original Sin takes place at the very moment that Adam disobeys the command—but it is apparent in the effects that the sin has on Adam and Eve themselves; it is seen at work in the transmission of the sin to all posterity with the voluntary participation by that posterity; and it is evident in the various effects that it has on Adam and Eve's descendants.[1] The Genesis narrative, which was the doctrinal source for both Augustine and Milton, clearly taught that two conditions were necessary for the occurrence of transgression in the first place: a command given by God, whose authority and right to command are supreme (Gen. ii.17: "Thou shalt not eat of it"), and a deliberate and conscious transgression by the one who is bound by the command (Gen. iii.6: "She took of the fruit thereof and did eat and gave also unto her husband with her, and he did eat"). The two conditions are mentioned repeatedly in Chapters XI and XII of Milton's *Christian Doctrine*. In the epic, God himself, without the use of any delegate (as if to impress Adam of the enormity of the issues involved), warns Adam immediately at the moment of his creation: "Remember what I warn thee, shun to taste, / And shun the bitter consequence" (VIII.327–28); and, after the Fall, the Son in his God-man office pronounces: "Because thou hast heark'n'd to the voice of thy Wife, / And eaten of the Tree concerning which / I charg'd thee, saying: Thou shalt not eat thereof, / Curs'd is the ground for thy sake, thou in sorrow / Shalt eat thereof all the days of thy Life" (X.198–202).

Augustine emphasizes the lightness of the command and the ease with which it might have been observed, despite the seriousness of the consequences. It was no mere disobedience of a moral

42

precept; it was a grave sin because of the circumstances surrounding its committal. Adam had been explicitly commanded, and he had been warned from the moment of his creation as to the consequences of transgression. There could be no plea of a lack of knowledge. Moreover, the act of disobedience, performed by one in such a singularly privileged supernatural and preternatural state whereby nothing was wanting, must have been sheer rebellion of the mind and will against the ultimate supernatural claims and rights of God. Augustine maintains that the command enjoining abstinence from one kind of food in the midst of a great abundance of other kinds was an extremely light one and required very little effort to observe. Therefore, the iniquity of violating it was all the greater in proportion to the ease with which it might have been kept.[2] Adam's awareness of this is evident in his first speech in Book IV. He reminds Eve that they have "no other service than to keep / This one, this easy charge, of all the Trees / In Paradise" (IV.420-22). This is not the first time that Adam speaks after his creation, but it is the first time that the reader hears him. We are immediately aware of Adam's cognizance of the lightness of the command, the ease with which it can be observed, and, therefore, the outright deliberation on his part in Book IX to violate it. Also, the first and original sin, which Augustine calls "peccatum ineffabiliter grande," was a free, personal transgression; precisely as Adam had been warned, all generations would inherit a state of sin because of his personal transgression (Gen. iii.16: "In sorrow thou shalt bring forth children"). There may have been ease in the observance of the command, but there certainly was no levity of matter here. Adam speaks of "One easy prohibition" (IV.433), but he is very much aware from the beginning, and reminded by Raphael, of all that is involved in his responsibility.

Considering the privileged status of the progenitors and the enormous consequences involved, Milton, like centuries of thinkers before him, never questioned the seriousness or culpability of Adam's sin. Concerning its gravity, Augustine says:

> There is in it pride, because man chose to be under his own dominion rather than under the dominion of God; and sacrilege, because he did not believe in God; and murder, because he brought death upon himself; and spiritual fornication, because the purity of the human mind was cor-

rupted by the seducing blandishments of the serpent; and theft, for man turned to his own use the food he had been forbidden to touch; and avarice, for he had a craving for more than should have been sufficient for him, and whatever other sin can be discovered upon careful reflection to be involved in this one admitted sin.[3]

Milton, as if to echo Augustine, says:

Anyone who examines this sin carefully will admit, and rightly, that it was a most atrocious offence, and that it broke every part of the law. For what fault is there which man did not commit in committing this sin? He was to be condemned both for trusting Satan and for not trusting God; he was faithless, ungrateful, disobedient, greedy, uxorious; she, negligent of her husband's welfare; both of them committed theft, robbery with violence, murder against their children (i.e. the whole human race); each was sacrilegious and deceitful, cunningly aspiring to divinity, although thoroughly unworthy of it, proud and arrogant.[4]

The cataloging of offenses is not new or peculiar to Augustine and Milton; indeed, it was a commonplace of traditional Christian theology, and such enumerating can be found in most reputable commentators on Original Sin. But the catalog in *Christian Doctrine* and its dramatic presentation in the epic at the time of the temptation and immediately after the Fall do bring home, all the more forcefully, the facts that Milton was careful to stay within the mainstream of Christian thought and that his teaching on Original Sin was very thorough and well defined. Moreover, his placing disobedience only fourth in the catalog should tell us much of what Milton thought constituted the sin. Modern critics have defined it as lack of humility, uxoriousness, sensuality, triviality of mind, comradeship, and idolatry. But the catalog and the epic presentation of it tell us that the whole law was involved here and not simply one particular sin. E. L. Marilla's observation, made in 1953, that their defection was a "defiance of the whole divine plan in the cosmic scheme of things," is still the best definition of what happened in Eden.[5] Since the whole law is involved, enormous issues are involved with enormous consequences; and Adam's culpability is all the greater as a result, in spite of the fact that—indeed, because of it—there was such ease in observing the prohibition.

The immediate effect produced in Adam and Eve by sin was that they lost their gifts of divine grace, immortality, impassibility, and integrity. Man's mortality is a direct result of Adam's first sin (Gen. ii.17: "In the day that thou eatest thereof thou shalt surely die"), and this is reiterated time and time again by both Augustine and Milton. Adam's body was regarded by Augustine as capable of either death or immortality. The natural law of death was conditionally suspended, and Adam's body was such that it was not necessary that it should die. But with the transgression the conditional promise of immortality was cancelled, and death came into the world. Mortality is man's punishment for disobedience and is therefore called sin, but Augustine is careful to assert that no one sins simply by dying; it is called sin because it is the punishment for sin.[6] Throughout his works, Augustine speaks of the various types of death; but in treating Adam and Eve and the first fall, he invariably refers to death in terms of bodily mortality.

In Milton's very systematic treatment of death in *Christian Doctrine* (Chapters XII, XIII, XXVII), we see it in its various degrees and in its larger meaning. He begins by asserting that "in Scripture every evil, and everything which seems to lead to destruction, is indeed under the name of death. For physical death, as it is called, did not follow on the same day as Adam's sin, as God had threatened."[7] Consequently, death means not only the mortality of the body, but also the loss of freedom from pain and of integrity. This is a very interesting point that Milton makes, particularly in respect to "everything which seems to lead to destruction," because, as we have seen, the immortality of the body with which Adam had been endowed necessarily excluded all those sufferings and infirmities which lead to death. Consequently, because of the intimate relationship of the preternatural gifts, Milton finds it impossible to speak of the loss of one without speaking of the loss of the other. He points out that the first degree of death comprehends "All evils which tend to death and which, it is agreed, came into the world as soon as man fell"[8]—in other words, all those things from which, by virtue of their immortality, the gift of freedom from pain and suffering had preserved Adam and Eve.

In the epic, he speaks of "Death into the World, and all our woe" (I.3), "into a World / Of woe and sorrow" (VIII.332–33), and "Misery / Death's Harbinger" (IX.12–13). And further, under the third degree of death, where he considers the death of the body, he includes again all those things from which Adam and Eve were secured by their freedom from pain and suffering: "The body's sufferings and hardships and diseases are nothing but the prelude to this bodily death."[9] In the epic, when Adam is allowed to see death for the first time in Cain and Abel, Michael says, "Death thou hast seen / In his first shape on man" (XI.466–67), and continues

> but many shapes
> Of Death, and many are the ways that lead
> To this grim Cave, all dismal; yet to sense
> More terrible at th' entrance than within.
> Some, as thou saw'st, by violent stroke shall die,
> By Fire, Flood, Famine, by Intemperance more
> In Meats and Drinks, which on the Earth shall bring
> Diseases dire....
>
> (XI.467–74)

It is very significant that Milton should treat death in this fashion. The loss of grace, freedom from pain, and integrity took place at the moment of transgression; while death, in its limited sense of bodily death, did not. And yet death is the effect most closely associated with the transgression, and the threat of death was the primary penalty of which the progenitors had been warned. So utmost was it in the poet's mind that it is alluded to innumerable times in the epic. The poet had a very definite teaching on the freedom from pain and suffering; and death, which seems to be the primary preoccupation of any speaker when he refers to the Fall, is all the evils and everything which, in its consequence, leads to death. This approach to death, which is so theologically sound, was very important for Milton's dramatic purpose. It is nonsense to conclude that Milton himself was at a loss in the epic to explain why Adam and Eve continue living after their transgression. Milton had a wide body of teaching on death at his disposal—a teaching that was ever on the lips of the pulpit preachers (for example, John Donne); a teaching that was a favorite of seventeenth-century Scriptural commentators and doctrinal writers—and he could presume that his reader was educated enough to understand death, with its various degrees, in its wider connotation. Such a sophisticated view contributes to the wide breadth of knowledge, the vast scope of doctrinal teaching, that is so much a part of epic decorum, particularly in an epic whose framework is embedded in the vast Christian tradition.

Under the second degree of death, Milton discusses Adam's loss of sanctity.[10] That the soul becomes spiritually dead at the moment of grave sin is a far more traditional understanding of death and a commonplace teaching in Christian theology. That Adam and Eve lost their sanctity, with a consequent weakening of their rational faculties, is at the very root of Augustinian teaching on Original Sin and Redemption. One of the most important themes running throughout *Paradise Lost* is that Jesus Christ, the second Adam, will come to regain what the first Adam had lost, and that through his redemptive and re-creative works, mankind will be revivified by grace and become, by adoption, the sons of God. So prominent in Milton's mind was this theme that it is stated in the opening lines of the epic, "till one greater Man / Restore us" (I.4-5). Adam's condition, through grace, constituted a special relationship with God. This higher life postulates and implies conformity between man's mind and will and God's, for it consists in the close union of the soul and the soul's activity with divine life.[11] Where there is a division of wills, there cannot be oneness of life. Adam, therefore, by putting his will in opposition to God's (Eph. iv.18: "Being alienated from the life of God"), deprived himself necessarily of this union with and sharing in the divine life.[12] He had, at the moment of transgression, become spiritually dead. Concerning this spiritual death, Milton says: "The second degree of death is called Spiritual Death. This is the loss of that divine grace and innate righteousness by which, in the beginning, man lived with God."[13] This death, unlike the death of the body, took place at the moment of the Fall. In the epic, immediately after the Fall, we see

> innocence, that as a veil
> Had shadow'd them from knowing ill, was gone,

47

Just confidence, and native righteousness,
And honour from about them.

(IX.1054-57)

As a consequence of the loss of grace, there is a change or a weakening in men's faculties; the reason is obscured, which in turn weakens the understanding.[14] "For Understanding rul'd not, and the Will / Heard not her lore" (IX.1127-28), and there is a deprivation of freedom.[15]

Another effect of the loss of grace is that which Milton terms "peccatis cumulantur," and which the Yale edition translates "sins are heaped upon sins." Actually, the aspect of habitual sin is one of the most important facets of the doctrine of Original Sin. Adam's sin was a personal sin, and insofar as it was personal, it could not fall on his descendants. What is transmitted to his descendants is the state of sin, not the act, and this state is called habitual sin. Milton does not give the term its closer theological meaning, that is, permanence or fixity in a condition of sinfulness which results from the commission of the one sin. More modern theologians understand habitual sin as some sinful act committed so often that it has become an acquired habit, such as habitually lying or drinking to excess. It is this more modern sense that Milton favors, for he speaks of the increasing amount of sins which makes the sinner more vile and destitute after the loss of grace.[16] In *Paradise Lost* this is quite evident when Adam and Eve, weakened by the first sin, follow the inclination of the will and a series of sins follows. Milton uses the authority of Paul (Rom. i.26) for the proof of habitual sin—the "propterea tradidit eos foedis affectibus" passage, which means that God permitted men to follow their own free will which, when weakened by sin, invariably follows the inclination to evil. Milton understands "peccatis cumulantur" to mean the propensity to repeated sin which man has because he is weakened by the original fall, rather than the state of sin itself. Both definitions of habitual sin are found in Augustine: one as the permanent or fixed sinful state itself; the other as man's inclinations or acts in the sinful state.

By Original Sin, Adam and Eve lost their gift of integrity. Adam's flesh was originally obedient to the spirit, but after the Fall, concupiscence had full sway, and all mankind derived from him this concupiscence of the flesh. This defect was unknown before the first sin. Despite the fact that Adam and Eve enjoyed the pleasures of the sensitive life, they did not experience the conflict of disobedient lust. This affliction came about because of the first disobedience. As they rebelled, so they experienced the rebellion of their flesh. Before his fall, man had no occasion to feel ashamed; after his fall, he felt the need to hide his shame. Concerning this novelty, Augustine says: "But when they were stripped of this grace, that their disobedience might be punished by fit retribution, there became in the movement of their bodily members a shameless novelty which made nakedness indecent; it at once made them observant and made them ashamed."[17]

In his treatment of Original Sin, Milton uses the term "concupiscence" in its widest and most general sense, which, while not necessarily erroneous, can lead to difficulties. In discussing the actual fall and the sin of Adam and Eve, he distinguishes between Original Sin, or that sin which is common to all,[18] and personal sin, which "each man commits on his own account, quite apart from that sin which is common to all."[19] Both of these sins, the original and the personal, consist of two elements: evil concupiscence, or the desire of sinning (*concupiscentia mala seu male faciendi libido*); and the act of sinning itself (*et malefactum ipsum*).[20] He then proceeds to define concupiscence as "evil desire that our first parents were guilty of. Then they implanted it in all their posterity, since their posterity too was guilty of that original sin, in the shape of a certain disposition towards, or, to use a metaphor, a sort of tinder to kindle sin."[21] The phrase "Quam primi parentis et in se primum admiserunt" is apt to lead to difficulties because evil concupiscence, as it is an effect of Original Sin, might be understood as being the very nature of Original Sin. The definition must be considered in the light of Milton's comments on Original Sin in the beginning of Chapter XI of the treatise. After defining Original Sin, Milton explains that this sin originated, firstly, in the instigation of the devil, and, secondly, in the liability to fall with which man was created.[22] Because of this liability, Adam is able to choose; and if he chooses, he does so because he desires to. It is not unusual to find theologians, including Augustine, associating concupiscence so closely with Original Sin. After all, the term concupiscence does carry with it the meaning of "desire," and if Adam

and Eve were free and liable and, despite all warnings, took of
the apple, such an act implies that their wills desired to do so.
Consequently, this "primi parentis et in se primum admiserunt"
can only mean that our original parents were guilty of desiring
as they did, and that was to be disobedient. Concupiscence here
cannot mean unbridled passion, because Milton refers too often
to the Fall as an outright act of disobedience rather than one of
passion.

One of the earliest and most obvious effects of the Fall in *Paradise Lost*, an effect which was most significant for Milton, is
Adam and Eve's lust, into which they fall with such abandon. It
is the most dominant effect of the Fall, but it is not the prime sin
itself. Therefore, the concupiscence of which Adam and Eve
were first guilty was that of choosing as they did, which is quite
different from the concupiscence which comes from the loss of
integrity, and which, in turn, sets off a host of passions. It is this
latter sense of the term with which the doctrine of Original Sin
is concerned. Eve's eating the apple released the guard of integrity, and the series of incidents that follows shows us concupiscence in various forms. There is Eve's ambition, "nor was
God-head from her thought" (IX.790); her gluttony, "Greedily
she ingorg'd without restraint" (IX.791); and her desire for
equality, "the more to draw his Love, / And render me more
equal" (IX.822-23). Physical indications of the loss of integrity
can be seen in Eve, as she rushes to Adam with a guilty conscience: "in her face excuse / Came Prologue" (IX.853-54), and
again, "in her Cheek distemper flushing glow'd" (IX.887); and
in the two of them: "our Faces evident the signs/Of foul concupiscence" (IX.1077-78). They felt shame with their new state:

> Some Tree whose broad smooth Leaves together sew'd,
> And girded on our loins may cover round
> Those middle parts, that this new comer, Shame,
> There sit not, and reproach us as unclean.
> (IX.1095-98)

And all the passions became disobedient:

> nor only Tears
> Rain'd at thir Eyes, but high Winds worse within

Began to rise, high Passions, Anger, Hate,
Mistrust, Suspicion, Discord, and shook sore
Thir inward State of Mind.

(IX.1121-25)

There are the mutual accusations which close Book IX
(1134-86); and, finally, there is guilt, "and shame, and perturba-
tion, and despair, / Anger, and obstinacy, and hate, and guile"
(X.113-14), and the terror of conscience which accompanies
guilt—"O Conscience, into what Abyss of fears / And horrors
hast thou driv'n me" (X.842-43), and "Which to his evil Conscience represented / All things with double terror" (X.849-50).
All of these are facets of concupiscence, but the most impressive
indication of the loss of integrity is the scene of carnal lust:

but that false Fruit
Far other operation first display'd,
Carnal desire inflaming, hee on Eve
Began to cast lascivious Eyes, she him
As wantonly repaid; in Lust they burn.

(IX.1011-15)

Milton's method of portraying pre-lapsarian Eve and Adam as
exhibiting virtues which later turn into corresponding vices
makes the most striking contrast in the portrayal of the marital
act in Book VIII and Book IX. The act is the same, but in Book
IX the circumstances are different, vastly different. Through the
contrast, Milton is showing that, as Augustine taught, man's
disobedience to himself is what he merits for disobedience to
God.

One of the major problems associated with the doctrine of
Original Sin was the question of the relationship of the sin to
human nature. In other words, what is the nature of man in
terms of the context of Original Sin? We have seen that Adam
and Eve's condition at the beginning of their lives was one of
supernatural and preternatural prerogatives, and we have seen
that because of their disobedience these endowments were lost. If
these endowments were natural to Adam, or a constitutive part
of his created human nature, then, since by his sin he lost them
both for himself and for posterity, it will follow that man's

nature now is intrinsically and essentially vitiated by being deprived of some elements originally proper to it; it will therefore be, in itself, an evil thing. If, on the other hand, these endowments were something given to Adam over and above all that went to make up his full manhood, then it follows that, in spite of their loss, human nature remains complete—in essence, unimpaired by Original Sin; intrinsically whole and good in itself. The delicacy of the problem lies in determining with accuracy what is meant by the term "human nature."

In a strict theological sense, human nature (or the nature of man) means the sum total of the elements that make a man the kind of creature he is, namely, a rational (reasoning) animal. These elements are a body and a rational soul. The body gives animality; the soul gives him rationality; the union of the two makes him a rational animal. These two elements constitute his nature, and from the union of these two arise certain powers, faculties, and properties. He is capable of manual work and intellectual work; he can achieve improvements in his environment; he can utilize to his advantage the materials he finds around him. Being a rational animal, he possesses reason and free will; he may know God as God can be known by reason; and he is capable of performing acts of natural virtue. God might have left man thus, without conferring a higher gift, for it would not have been unjust to create man in a state of pure nature. So created, he would have been subject to disease, suffering, and death, to ignorance and the rebellion of the appetites. He would have been destitute of grace and could never have hoped for the happiness of heaven. But, at the same time, he would have had the ordinary help of God's providence to assist him in avoiding sin and doing his duty; and, if faithful to the natural law, he would have had his reward in knowing God eternally, insofar as he could be known by reason. Such a state was possible.

God, however, poured into Adam's and Eve's souls the unique gift which transcends all nature, sanctifying grace.[23] This state of grace was in accordance with Adam's nature, for the supernatural ennoblement and perfection of human nature is not unnatural or "contra naturam" but is entirely in accordance with and befitting nature.[24] Yet this gift exceeded the demands and powers of his given nature, and was one completely undue his created

52

nature.[25] Consequently, the loss of the gift was the loss of something befitting his nature, but not the loss of something that was originally proper to it. Adam's immortality was, in reality, only potential, not actual—that is, it was something that would have been given him if he had observed the conditions accompanying God's promise of it, but of which he was deprived owing to his failure to observe them. Therefore, while death was truly a penalty for Adam's sin, it was a penalty that consisted in not giving a conditionally promised additional privilege but not in taking away something already held by natural right.[26] Death, therefore, was Adam's natural lot; immortality was not natural to him. Consequently, the loss of the gift did not affect that which was natural to him, his human nature. The gift of integrity protected man from concupiscence; but it must be pointed out that concupiscence is a natural effect of man's dual nature, of his having two kinds of appetites—sensitive and rational. Between the objects of sense and of reason, there must often, of necessity, be opposition; and since the sensitive faculties and appetites are directly, easily, and strongly excited and stimulated by external objects, it comes about inevitably that they begin to act without the cooperation and consent of reason, and that sometimes they act so forcefully as to put the reason to great stress before it can impose its power and control. Concupiscence is a natural concomitant of man's composite being, and integrity was over and above his human nature. Such immunity from concupiscence was not natural; it was a privilege, a preternatural gift with which God endowed the head of the human race. Thus, concupiscence, like death, was natural to man; and the loss of the gift placed man back into his natural state.

All of this, of course, is not to belittle the gravity of the deprivation of the gifts in question. Though they were not natural to Adam, they were an endowment and perfection of his whole being, raising him to a higher level, giving him new capacities, and setting up a natural harmony between all the elements of his nature. Therefore their loss, while not depriving him of any natural perfection and while leaving his manhood intact and unspoilt in itself, left his being without all those added ornaments and graces which gave it such strength and beauty. If the gifts were a constitutive element of his human nature, then it would follow that Adam's nature would be intrinsically depraved and corrupted, and a thing evil in itself. It would mean that every human act is of itself and in itself evil, for it would spring from an evil nature. Consequently, his reason and free will would be destroyed, for he would be unable to choose to do good. All natural virtue would be impossible for him. The Christian tradition has never taught such a fatal doctrine. Adam indeed lost, by his sin, all his supernatural and preternatural gifts, but he did not lose anything belonging to his nature as man. All the elements, properties, and endowments that constituted his manhood, he kept intact. So, also, the human nature that he handed on to his children was perfect of its kind.

It is somewhat difficult to discern just how Augustine and Milton felt about Adam's human nature after the transgression, because both thinkers often insist that the whole man was corrupted by Original Sin. Augustine says of Adam and Eve that "the greatness of their crime depraved their nature,"[27] but it is important to understand just what Augustine means by nature, a term he often used in different contexts with different meanings. In order to understand Augustine's thinking on this matter, as on so many other things, one must consider that his intellectual life was a very dynamic one; and in order to understand a particular teaching, one must take an inclusive view of his whole range of mental development. Nature can mean essence, but it can also mean the whole of what something is, that is, essence and accidents; and it is this latter meaning that Augustine attributes to the word. As William Grace has pointed out, it was the late medieval commentators on Augustine who attributed to him the meaning of essence only;[28] authentic Augustinianism taught that nature was the whole man, essence and accidents. Grace continues: "Actually, the nature of something could be 'depraved' in the sense that its accidents had been injured. Man could have lost a position in Paradise that related to his total nature without his essence being affected. He has real losses, but he remains essentially man."[29]

When we understand that Augustine considered nature to include accidents, we then can better understand his use of the terms "vitium" and "vitiatum," concepts that he used often and sometimes synonymously. In treating Original Sin and human nature, however, he treats them as two different concepts. *Vitium*, he tells us, is that which is evil, and *vitiatum* is that which is faulty and impaired. Regardless of his insistence upon the whole man being affected by Original Sin, he is careful to guard himself against the charge that human nature is totally corrupted. He insists that human nature is not a "vitium" but a "vitiatum"—that is, human nature is diminished by a blemish or defect, and this is the result of an attack on its integrity, beauty, and virtue.[30] Consequently, Augustine feels that the gifts were not so much a part of man's human nature as to render that nature a *vitium* with their loss, but were, on the other hand, seated deep in his nature to the point that their loss simply diminished the strength and beauty of that nature. In maintaining that man's human nature is blemished or weakened by Original Sin, Augustine differs from present-day theologians who favor the view that Adam's manhood was kept totally intact and unspoilt; but what is most important is that the Father keeps within the Christian tradition with his insistence on the fundamental concept that Adam's human nature had not become totally corrupted by the Fall. It is here that I must part ways with Professor J. M. Evans in his reading of Augustine. Evans asserts that the depravity of the human will was, for Augustine, an effect of the Fall of Man. I think more consideration must be given to Augustine's concept of "depravity" and the distinction that he makes between "vitium" and "vitiatum." Evans's treatment of Milton and his debt to Augustine is excellent, but here he seems to neglect distinctions that Augustine often made in the whole body of his works.[31]

Milton lists the effects of the loss of grace as the obscuration of right reason, the deprivation of righteousness and liberty, the slavish subjection to sin and death (which is death to the will), and, finally, habitual sin. However, almost immediately, he qualifies this with: "It cannot be denied that some traces of the divine image still remain in us, which are not wholly extinguished by this spiritual death. This is quite clear, not only from the holiness and wisdom in both word and deed of the heathens, but also from Gen. ix 2: every beast shall have fear of you, and ix 6: who shed man's blood . . . because God made man in his image."[32] Consequently, even with the loss of grace and death to the soul, man who was made in the image of God still manifests some of the good of that divine image—indeed, even heathens. From this first indication in *Christian Doctrine*, it

55

seems that Milton did not consider man to have become basically corrupted. In this passage we see not only that every act of man is not necessarily evil because of his fall, but also that natural virtue is quite possible for him. Milton continues by stating that these vestiges of original excellence can be seen in man's understanding, which is capable of hearing and seeing,[33] and in the liberty of the will, which is not entirely destroyed. And if the liberty of the will is not destroyed, then "freedom has clearly not quite disappeared even where good works are concerned, or at least good attempts, at any rate after God has called us and given us grace."[34] He states further: "As a vindication of God's justice, especially when he calls man, it is obviously fitting that some measure of free will should be allowed to man, whether this is something left over from his primitive state, or something restored to him as a result of the call of grace. It is also fitting that this will should operate in good works or at least good attempts, rather than in things indifferent."[35] Whether or not Milton was consciously concerned with this problem of Adam's human nature after the Fall cannot be proved from *Christian Doctrine*, because the teaching is given no explicit systematic treatment in the treatise. Yet it must be pointed out that, in dealing with fallen man, he repeatedly insists on the freedom of the will, the capability of performing acts of natural virtue, the gift of reason still retained, and the fact that "everyone is provided with a sufficient degree of innate reason for him to be able to resist evil desires by his own effort; so no one can add strength to his excuse by complaining that his own nature is peculiarly depraved."[36] Time and time again, he reiterates that in fallen man there are still remnants of the divine image. These properties and powers are completely incompatible with an evil nature.

In *Paradise Lost*, from the moment of the Fall to the end of the epic, Milton never loses sight of the fact that man, who was derived from the substance of God, still retains remnants of the Divine Nature: "Why should not Man, / Retaining still Divine similitude / In part, from such deformities be free, / And for his Maker's Image sake exempt?" (XI.511–14). Certain acts of Adam and Eve in their state of sin can be interpreted only as acts of natural virtue, because at this point they are stripped of all that is supernatural and preternatural. For example, Adam's resignation, "If here would end / The misery, I deserv'd it, and would bear / My own deservings" (X.725-27); his preoccupation with his progeny, "But this will not serve; / All that I eat or drink, or shall beget, / Is propagated curse" (X.727-29); Eve's humble repentance (X.914-36); and Adam's forgiveness, which is not only an act of charity but a plea for charity: "But rise, let us no more contend, nor blame / Each other, blam'd enough elsewhere, but strive / In offices of Love" (X.958-60). In disapproving Eve's suggestion of self-inflicted death and continence, Adam advises prayer and faith in God's mercy, so that "both confess'd / Humbly thir faults, and pardon begg'd, with tears / Watering the ground, and with thir sighs the Air / Frequenting, sent from hearts contrite" (X.1100-3). Even before Adam is allowed the vision of the future, "from the Mercy-seat above / Prevenient Grace descending had remov'd / The stony from thir hearts, and made new flesh / Regenerate grow instead" (XI.2-5). This grace, of course, is not the same as the grace they once had and which will return in virtue of the promise. This is divine assistance which is given to a sinner before repentance.[37]

The fact that Milton has so many incidents of sorrow and repentance even before Adam is allowed the vision which will reveal to him the good to come from the *felix culpa* indicates that Adam can still make right use of his reason and free will, which, otherwise, would be impossible if his human nature were now evil. He also has the help of "providence thir guide" to assist him in his duty, which Providence would be useless to a corrupt human nature. Michael tells Adam: "God is as here, and will be found alike / Present, and of his presence many a sign / Still following thee" (XI.350-53); and Adam realizes he will be "As in his presence, ever to observe / His Providence, and on him sole depend" (XII.563-64). If Michael advises, "add Faith, / Add Virtue, Patience, Temperance, add Love / By name to come call'd Charity, the soul / Of all the rest" (XII.582-85), for in this way "A paradise within thee, happier far" (XII.587) will be found, then fallen man must have a nature conditioned to receive it.

The aspect of corporate unity or co-inherence in the sin of Adam is one that presented no problem to Milton. Augustine, like most of the patrological writers, held that the sin of Adam is transmitted and inheres as a true sin in all his descendants (Gen. iii.16: "Through the offense of one many are dead").[38] He says,

"For we were all in that one man, when we were all that one man who through a woman fell into sin."[39] Milton, after defining Original Sin, gives a lengthy treatment to the aspect of participation of Adam's progeny in the first sin. But the difficulty arises as to how this state of deprivation in which Adam's descendants are born—this loss of original justice—can be said to be sinful, when sin is essentially a matter of free will. An explanation of this fact requires a return to the basic understanding of what God's will was from the beginning. It was God's will that Adam should be physically and juridically the head of the human race and, as such, should act as its representative. Augustine maintains that God did not create Eve, who was to be Adam's wife, as he created Adam, but created her out of man so that the whole human race might be derived from one man.[40] God had given Adam original justice and its concomitant preternatural prerogatives, not only as a personal heritage, but as a heritage which he was to transmit to all his descendants. In other words, original justice was essentially hereditary justice; and it follows that immortality was essentially hereditary immortality and a privilege given to the human race as such.[41] Hereditary grace was related to human nature from the first by the free will of God. When Adam renounced original justice, he acted not for himself alone but as the representative of his race, as the moral juridical head of the whole human family. Thus, the loss of original justice was essentially a privation of hereditary justice and, as such, was tantamount to a voluntary renunciation on the part of human nature of its supernatural heritage. The voluntary renunciation involves an hereditary guilt, which is voluntary on the part of each and every human being.[42] Consequently, Original Sin is not a personal sin, but a sin of nature, conditioned upon our generic relation to Adam, who, contrary to the will of God, despoiled human nature of grace and thereby rendered it hostile to its creator.

Milton makes this quite explicit with his distinction between Original Sin and personal sin. The personal sin involves desire and act and is performed through words, thoughts, and occasions.[43] Original Sin, however, is that which is passed on to Adam's progeny and which is voluntary through the act of the first parents. It is voluntary through our relationship and solidarity with and spiritual dependence upon Adam. Milton says,

"For Adam, the parent and head of all men, either stood or fell as a representative of the whole human race: this was true both when the covenant was made, that is, when he received God's commands, and also when he sinned."[44] When Adam renounced original justice, which was intended for all and to be passed on to all, he lost it for all—"And in them all their posterity: for they are judged and condemned in them, although not yet born, Gen. iii, 16, etc., so they must obviously have sinned in them as well."[45]

In *Paradise Lost*, Adam had been made aware of this grave responsibility by Raphael—"Thine and of all thy Sons / The weal or woe in thee is plac't; beware" (VIII.637-38)—and after the fall, the realization of mankind's participation in the transgression intensifies his remorse: "Fair Patrimony / That I must leave ye, Sons; O were I able / To waste it all myself, and leave ye none!" (X.818-20). Death, which means the loss of all the privileges, comes not only to Adam but to all mankind: "He with his whole posterity must die" (III.209), and "suffering death, / The penalty of thy transgression due, / And due to theirs which out of thine will grow" (XII.398-400). For Milton there is no problem in the severity of God's justice concerning transmission. He says, "It is not only a constant principle of divine justice but also a very ancient law among all races and religions, that when a man has committed sacrilege (and this tree we are discussing was sacred), not only he but also the whole of his posterity becomes anathema and a sin-offering."[46] The examples Milton uses—the Deluge, the destruction of Sodom, the burning of Jericho, Agag and his people suffering for the crime of his father, the whole of Egypt smitten for the offense of Pharoah—are characteristic of the examples used by theologians who have attempted to give a theological proof for this dogma from reason. Like all analogies between the human and the divine, it falls short of being an adequate picture of the reality; but, as far as it goes, the illustration is good and important, for it shows that generations have seldom recognized corporate unity on a human level as an injustice to mankind.

The mystery of corporateness, co-inherence or unity, which Milton never questioned and which is a persistent one in the history of Christian theology, has been greatly neglected, especially when we consider that *Paradise Lost*, as an epic, is dealing with the whole Christian plan of salvation. Books XI and XII of the epic have, from the first, been regarded by most readers as less completely realized in terms of sensory detail—this fact is mentioned by Addison in his *Spectator* papers on these books. As a matter of fact, some critics think the books should never have been included, because after the Fall they seem to be anti-climactic. But the plan of salvation did not end with the Fall of Man. In fact, the plan reaches its finality in the rise of man; and if there has ever been any question of the justification for Books XI and XII, aside from the fact that they are essential to the architectural balance of the epic, the answer is in the fact that they are the fulfillment of this plan.[47] In these books, not only do we see the sin of Adam transmitted, but we also see it at work. We see in Adam's sin the unity of all the fallen individuals who share in the common human nature form; and in the promised Redemption, we see the unity of the restored humanity in Christ. For Augustine, it is in this "in pluribus unitas" that we see God's justice and God's love. Adam's fall was our fall, and Christ's restoration was our restoration.

CHAPTER 5

Redemption

The final phase in the plan of salvation is the Redemption, and the Redemption in Milton's scheme is, as it was for theologians centuries before him, not only the culmination of this great plan but also the basis for many other dogmas of the Christian church which are developments of its consequences. For Milton, after treating the redemptive work of Christ in *Christian Doctrine*, discusses faith as an effect of man's supernatural renovation. Faith, in turn, is a complete doctrinal teaching which traditional theologians term *De Fide*, and which Milton develops as *De Fide Salvifica*. Similarly, when Milton treats Christ as Mediator between God and man, he relates to his study of the Redemption his whole Christology, which of itself is a theological doctrine apart. The same can be said for his treatment of the Redeemer as king. The spiritual kingdom of Christ is the Church, and the Church again is a separate dogmatic study which theologians entitled *De Ecclesia* and Milton develops as *De Ecclesia Visibili*. In *Paradise Lost,* when we read "Baptizing in the profluent stream" (XII.442), Milton is speaking of the outward sign of one of the first fruits of the Redemption, and this entails a complete sacramental system, *De Sacramentis*, which Milton develops in Book I, Chapter XXVIII, of his treatise. Likewise, in the passage "who shall dwell / His Spirit within them" (XII.487-88), Michael refers to the coming of the Holy Spirit. The Holy Spirit is one of the first fruits of the Redemption, and around this concept has been constructed the whole Christian teaching *De Spiritu Sancto*. The Redemption, then, seen in relation to the whole of Christian theology, is actually the pivotal concept which links into a consistent whole the many branches of Christian doctrine.

In *Paradise Lost,* the Redemption is seen for what it is—the final step in the plan of salvation, the fulfillment of God's economy. No sooner are we told of the fall of Adam and Eve, "Of Man's First Disobedience" (I.1), than we are told of the promised Redeemer, "till one greater Man Restore us" (I.4-5). The story of salvation begins with the Original Sin of Adam and ends with the Redemption of the world. All men fell in Adam; all men are to rise in Christ. The redemptive act of Christ, then, is the final solution in the drama of mankind. To understand fully the restoring work of Christ, the various aspects of the doctrine of the Redemption must be distinguished. The fact of the Incarnation must be established, giving special consideration to the controversy surrounding the motivation for decreeing the Incarnation. The concept of Mediation must be examined from the point of view of Christ as Mediator, taking into consideration the three offices of the Mediator. And, finally, consideration must be given to the properties of the Redemption—adequate, universal, and superabundant—which reveal the perfection of the redemptive work.

The Incarnation

An investigation of Milton's doctrine of the Incarnation reveals that the poet's overall ideology is Augustinian.[1] The Incarnation is the act whereby the Divine Word, the only begotten Son of God, took to himself a true human nature[2] (John i.1,14: "The Word was God.... And the Word was made flesh"). In Milton's treatise, we read that "His nature is double, divine and human," and this is defined as "a mutual hypostatic union of two natures."[3] In the epic, God announces: "Thir Nature also to thy Nature join; / And be thyself Man among men on Earth" (III.282–83). In assuming a human nature, Christ was given a body, a natural soul, and all else that belongs essentially to man[4] (Luke xxiv.39: "Behold my hands and my feet, that it is I myself: handle me and see: for a spirit hath not flesh and bones, as you see me have"; and xxiii.46: "Into thy hands I commend my spirit"). Milton teaches that "The fact that Christ had a body shows that he was a real man...so does the fact that he had a soul...and a spirit."[5] This appears in the epic with Christ's words, "Thou wilt not leave me in the loathsome grave / His prey, nor suffer my unspotted Soul / For ever with corruption there to dwell" (III.247–49). Augustine teaches that, in his human nature, Christ was born of a Virgin Mother without having any man for a father[6] (Matt. i.20: "That which is conceived in her is of the Holy Ghost"); and Milton explains: "There are two parts to Christ's incarnation: the conception and the nativity. The efficient cause of the former was the Holy Spirit ... I should say that these words refer to the power and the spirit of the Father himself."[7] In the epic, we read: "A Virgin is his Mother, but his Sire / The Power of the most High" (XII.368-69).

The union of the two natures was such that each remained distinct from the other, having its own will and operation[8]; Milton says, "And there is nothing to stop the properties of each from remaining individually distinct."[9] When the Father assures the Son in Book III that "Nor shalt thou by descending to assume / Man's Nature, lessen or degrade thine own" (303-4), he is articulating an Augustinian teaching that Christ, in assuming a human nature, did not become degraded and did not lose any of his divine nature.[10] So in the God-man there is "one" person, the "one" person of God the Son.[11] Milton says: "It follows that the union of two natures in Christ was the mutual hypostatic union of two essences. Because where a perfect substantial essence exists, there must also be a hypostasis or subsistence, since they are quite evidently the same thing. So one Christ, one ens, and one person is formed from this mutual hypostatic union of two natures."[12] In the epic, God says, "This day I have begot whom I declare / My only Son" (V.603-4). The Son of God, thus made man, came to shed his blood and die on the cross[13] "at the price of his own blood"[14] (Acts xx.28: "The Church of God, which he hath purchased with his own blood"). In the epic, we are told: "The blood of Bulls and Goats, they may conclude / Some blood more precious must be paid for Man, / Just for unjust" (XII.292-94); and this blood-shedding was accepted by God as an atonement for the Original Sin of mankind[15] (Heb. ix.22: "Without shedding of blood is no remission"). Milton says, "Moreover God would not accept any other sacrifice, since any other would have been less worthy."[16] In the epic, he tells us: "So Man, as is most just, / Shall satisfy for Man, be judg'd and die" (III.294-95). So, through the merits of Christ, the race of man was raised from the state of fallen nature, and, being placed into a state of repaired nature, was capable of being admitted after death to the enjoyment of the supernatural life[17] (Rom. v.15: "For if through the offense of one many be dead, much more than grace of God, and the gift by grace,

which is by one man Jesus Christ, hath abounded unto many";
and v.17: "For if by one man's offense death reigned by one;
much more they which receive abundance of grace and of the
gift of righteousness shall reign in life by one, Jesus Christ").
Milton says, "Man's restoration is that act by which man, freed
from sin and death by God the Father through Jesus Christ, is
raised to a far more excellent state of grace and glory than that
from which he fell."[18] And this is repeated in the epic: "Next, to
the Son, / Destin'd restorer of Mankind, by whom / New Heav'n
and Earth shall to the Ages rise, / Or down from Heav'n de-
scend" (X.645–48).

The Incarnation, then, was the means whereby the Redemption was to be fulfilled. But determining the actual motive for
the Incarnation—that is, the soteriological aspects of the doctrine of the Redemption—presents a controversy that has
intrigued thinkers down through the ages, Milton not excluded.
The Incarnation was dictated by two principal motives: the glorification of Christ and compassion for the misery of mankind.
But the problem is, Which one of these two motives outweighed
the other? One school of thought places the Incarnation prior to
all else and independent of the Fall of Man; another places it
wholly contingent upon man's transgression. Those who posit
the Incarnation as occurring first conceive of the absolute predestination of Christ and his divine kingdom as primary to everything, including all other divine decrees, with the permission of
the sin of Adam and the mission of Christ as passible Redeemer
of mankind as secondary.[19] Those who relegate the Incarnation
to a secondary position hold that God created the universe without regard for Christ, decreed subsequently to permit sin, and,
lastly, determined on the Incarnation of the Logos for the purpose of redeeming the human race.[20]

The first school maintains that God's principal motive in
decreeing the Incarnation was the dignity and glorification of
Christ. The universe was created for Christ's sake; and even if
Adam had not sinned, Christ would have come in the capacity of
a kingly, glorified God-man. The strength of this position lies
in the argument that the end cannot be inferior to the means
devised for its attainment, that is, that the Incarnation merely
served the purpose of the Redemption. The other school ascribes
the Incarnation of the Logos primarily to God's mercy and

maintains that the Fall was an indispensable condition of the Incarnation. Interestingly, elements of both schools are found in the soteriology of Augustine and Milton. Augustine, along with several other Church Fathers, held, for example, that the nature of matrimony, as an image of Christ's union with his church (Eph. v.31ff: "For this cause shall a man leave his father and mother, and shall be joined unto his wife, and they two shall be one flesh. This is a great mystery: but I speak concerning Christ and the Church"), was revealed to Adam in Paradise—a position which implicitly argues in favor of the former school.[21] From this teaching, one can conclude that Augustine felt that Christ's appearance on earth must not be conceived as conditional upon the Fall. He says, "Even if man had not sinned but had remained in the state of innocence matrimony would still be a symbol of Christ's union with his Church."[22] If matrimony would still be a symbol of Christ's union with his church even in the state of innocence, then the incarnate Christ would necessarily have come regardless of the Fall. He would have come not as redeemer but as king and head of God's mystical and visible church. And, when Milton argues that "Christ is the head of the mystical church, so no one is rightly or can possibly be at the head of the visible church, except Christ,"[23] he is saying in effect that God's mystical church, regardless of what happened in Eden, existed from the beginning of creation and had Christ as its ordained head. God's church, then, as it existed in the preternatural state, had Christ as its head, just as God's church, in our post-lapsarian world, has Christ as its head.

The problem for a number of medieval and Renaissance theologians was whether there would have been a church if mankind had persevered in its unfallen state. There appears to be nothing in Milton's theology to indicate that the poet felt there would not be. In fact, commenting on the mystical and invisible church, Milton asserts: "The body of Christ is mystically one, so it follows that the communion of his members must be mystic. It need not be subject to spatial considerations: it includes people from many remote countries, and from all ages since the creation of the world."[24] The clause "since the creation of the world" certainly indicates that the Church, with Christ as its head, existed in the time of Adam and Eve's unfallen state, indeed before it; and if the marriage state was a symbol of Christ's union with his church, a teaching which Milton never questioned,[25] then the poet is giving serious consideration to the first school in the soteriological controversy and is arguing for the primacy of Christ. It is most unlikely that Milton would hold that God's church was a post-lapsarian fabrication, that its creation was occasioned by the fall of Adam, and that the leadership and kingship of Christ was wholly dependent upon the sin of Adam. Furthermore, when Milton teaches that unfallen Adam and Eve, if they had persevered, could have moved into heaven as perfect humans (VII.154–61)—a teaching peculiar to Bonaventure—it follows logically that Christ, the head of all creation, could easily and gloriously have come to unfallen earth without any particular redemptive mission. In another instance, Milton argues: "Through Christ all things were made, both in heaven and earth, even the angels. In the beginning he was the word. He was God with God, and although he was not supreme, he was the firstborn of all creation. It follows that he must have existed before his incarnation."[26] Here he calls upon a text of St. Paul which theologians of the first school use as the Scriptural basis for the primacy-of-Christ theory: "By him were all things created...and he is before all, and by him all things consist. And he is the head of the body, the Church; who is the beginning, the first born from the dead: that in all things he may hold preeminence" (Col. i.16 et seq.). The Pauline authority of the firstborn of every creature can only be interpreted by these theologians thus: that Christ holds first place in the divine economy, that the world of angels and men was reserved to the last, and that the Incarnation cannot have been subordinate to the Creation and Redemption but, on the contrary, must rank far above it. Indeed, Milton's awareness of this subtle teaching and his frequent allusions to this school of thought attest to the depth of his theological thinking. Yet nowhere in *Christian Doctrine* do we find the poet adopting this theory or giving it explicit treatment as a possible motive for the Incarnation. On the other hand, we cannot ignore the many references to "first born," "kingship," and "anointed king" in the treatise and the epic. All we can say, therefore, is that Milton, like the Patristics and unlike the medieval theologians who actually formulated it as a doctrine, was aware of the teaching at least to the point of having the attributes of "kingship" and "first born" lend added dimensions to his portrayal of Christ.

But, despite the many references to the first school in Augustine's and Milton's thought, the weight of the evidence from their works goes to the more traditional theory. Augustine's investigation of the Redemption and the motive for the Incarnation is based on the passage in *De Peccato Originali*, "The Lord Jesus Christ came for no other reason...but to save, free, redeem, and illumine mankind,"[27] and on a passage in the *Enchiridion*, which teaches that "Christ became incarnate that he might redeem."[28] The *Enchiridion, De Peccato Originali*, and *De Gratia Christi* contain lengthy discourses on the fall of Adam as being the chief motive that prompted God to decree the Incarnation. Milton's discussion of the Redemption in *Christian Doctrine* is based on the concept that the original sin of Adam occasioned the coming of the Redeemer. Concerning the purpose of the Incarnation, he says, "The aim of this miraculous conception was to evade the pollution of Adam's sin."[29] And, in discussing the manhood of Christ, he maintains that there are reasons given most distinctly in Scripture why Christ should be incarnate, and the six citations he uses from Paul's Epistles to the Hebrews and Corinthians all pertain to the fallen state of man as occasioning the Incarnation.[30] In *Paradise Lost*, Christ's mission is for the salvation of man: "Destin'd restorer of Mankind" (X.646) who "offer'd himself to die / For man's offense" (III.409-10). Yet the actual motive for the Incarnation can be found in the important passage,

> well thou know'st how dear
> To me are all my works, nor Man the least
> Though last created, that for him I spare
> Thee from my bosom and right hand, to save,
> By losing thee a while, the whole Race lost.
> (III.276-80)

Also, the sequence of events in Book III is simply a dramatization of this traditional theory. We have the Father and the Son discussing Satan's flight to Paradise; the Father explaining to the Son the Fall of Man, which has not yet taken place but exists in the Father's foreknowledge; and the Son insisting on his own Incarnation in order that he might atone for the Fall that is yet to come:

> Behold mee then, mee for him, life for life
> I offer, on mee let thine anger fall;
> Account mee man; I for his sake will leave
> Thy bosom.
>
> (III.236–39)

The first theory, which groups the whole of creation around the Godhead as the center of the universe, the highest and final revelation, the beginning and end of all things, recommends itself for its sublimity. But actually, it is a theory inspired by a transcendent idealism and one of which Milton, despite a certain sympathy for it, was probably most suspicious. The poet would have had some difficulty in reconciling this theory with his teaching on the attributes of God and God's decrees in *Christian Doctrine*. Milton warns readers to avoid the dangers that beset men who think of God in an "anthropopathetic" manner.[31] When in the natural order man examines some course of activity, he is forced to analyze, and to distinguish in his mind, his motives for acting, the incentives which prompted him to act, and the various aspects of the end he hoped to achieve by his activity. But this is invalid if it is applied too vigorously to God, whose activity and thinking are of an absolute wisdom and of transcending simplicity. Milton insists that: "It is absurd, then, to separate God's decree or intention from his eternal resolution and foreknowledge and give the former chronological priority. For God's foreknowledge is simply his wisdom under another name, or that idea of all things which, to speak in human terms, he had in mind before he decreed anything."[32]

The first theory, which implies that Adam's sin was a kind of intrusion or misfortune that upset the first set of plans God had made for man's happiness, is precisely the kind of chronological imposition on God's "eternal resolution" that Milton rejects. Milton felt that, as part of his absolute wisdom, God, in creating Adam and Eve, knew that Adam would sin; he also knew that he willed to redeem fallen man by the passion and death of his Son, and that by the obedience of his death Christ would merit supreme glory for himself as the Lord of all things in heaven and earth. God made a progressive revelation of his plan, but there was no progression in the plan. He gradually unfolded in a temporal sequence of different stages his one divine plan which we see realized in one long history. The absolute simplicity of God's being, acts, mind, and will transcend human being and activity, defy time and chronology. The first theory ignores the basic metaphysical principle that God does not know things, as men do, because they exist; on the contrary, things exist in the way they do, and are linked with each other as they are, simply because they are part of the simplicity of God's own being. In the light, then, of Milton's teaching on God's decrees—their oneness and eternity—the first theory would appear much too anthropomorphic in approach and would be contrary to traditional orthodoxy as found in Scripture, which teaches that God is one and his decrees are one and eternal.

The second view, however, conforms to the facts as we know them from tradition, as does *Paradise Lost*. It is more solidly entrenched in the Scriptures; and we can be certain that Milton, with such authority buttressing this view, would be quite prone to mark his approval. Invariably, in *Paradise Lost*, when Milton speaks of the Son incarnate, he points to the sin of Adam. But, more important, the whole plan of salvation upon which *Paradise Lost* rests—that all men fell in Adam and all men are to rise in Christ—is actually the second view stated in traditional Augustinian terms. Man (Adam) is at the center of the epic. *Paradise Lost* and this tradition in no way ignore the dignity and glorification of Christ. The epic takes these for granted and then goes on to recognize the great and immense value of man in God's economy. Certainly, without the Fall of Man, Christ would be the King of Creation; and, in a sense, it would be perfect for him to have this title in a sinless order. But the whole economy of salvation, which is recounted for us in Scripture and tradition and which is the primary concern of *Paradise Lost*, does not pertain to a sinless order. It pertains to a present order which has as its central concern the whole of fallen mankind.

Christ was given, from all eternity, the additional office of Redeemer as well as the office of King; consequently, he was given additional glory for an office that would demand a far greater expression of love. In the present and wider order of things, Christ is far more gloriously Lord of mankind, which he not only created but also redeemed as the Word Incarnate, than he would have been in a sinless and, in a sense, limited order of things. So the greatest of all Christ's titles is "Redeemer of the human race." Thus, to say that man's sin was the foreseen occasion of God's willing the Incarnation is not, in any way, to lessen the glory God willed to Christ as his Son. Indeed, it is an implementation of glory. In his absolute wisdom and eternity, God knew that sin was an intrinsic possibility to any created creature, man or angel, because of that creature's limitations; so it is erroneous to posit, in the traditional view, that God willed the Incarnation on the chance and almost unforeseen occasion of this event ever taking place. It was not chance or unforeseen; it was all a part of his eternal resolution. As God is love, all his works necessarily express his love for his creatures. The Incarnation, then, the highest act of love, takes upon itself all the more glory because it is a response to permitted sin and to the needs of mankind. This is the reality which prompted the Christian tradition to express its cry "O felix culpa," and this is the reality which provides the foundation for the doctrine of the Redemption in *Paradise Lost*.

The Offices of Mediation

Both Augustine and Milton hold, then, that the Son of God incarnate came into the world in order to act as Mediator in the great task of the Redemption. Mediation is a word that has always carried the meaning of Redemption with it, yet the implication of the two views are distinct. By mediation is meant an action which serves to reunite or reconcile two alien or opposing objects or powers. The Mediator will belong to both. When the term mediation is used with reference to Christ, then, it means that he, the God-man, was able to reconcile men with God. The manner in which this reconciliation took place is better expressed in the term Redemption rather than Mediation, for Mediation might suggest that Christ was a kind of intermediary in nature, halfway between divine and human. Such a conception would be in complete opposition to the ideology of Augustine and of Milton, for both thinkers maintain Christ was fully

human and divine. Augustine's whole conception is based on
the fact that it was God who was offended and it was man who
offended; consequently, the Mediator could only be a God-man
(Acts iv.12: "Neither is there salvation in any other : for there is
none other name under heaven given among men, whereby we
must be saved"; and I Tim. ii.5: "For there is one God, and one
Mediator between God and men, the man Christ Jesus"). The
very circumstances of the transgression made it impossible for a
mere man to be the Mediator, or for a mere God to be the Mediator. Augustine says: "He is the Mediator between God and man
because He is God with the Father, and man with man. A mere
man could not be mediator between God and man; nor could a
mere God. Behold the Mediator: divinity without humanity cannot be mediator, nor humanity without divinity, but the human
divinity and the divine humanity of Christ is the sole mediator
between divinity and humanity."[33] He says further: "Christ is
the Mediator (between God and man) not because he is the word,
being immortal and happy in the highest degree, is far removed
from the miseries of mortal man, but he is the Mediator as
man."[34] For Milton, the Mediator sent into the world is Christ:
"Christ is the only redeemer or Mediator";[35] and, in the epic, he
says that the whole redemption of mankind would have been
lost "had not the Son of God, / In whom the fulness dwells of
love divine, / His dearest mediation thus renew'd" (III.224-26).
The suitability of Christ as Mediator is most apparent in Book
III of the epic. The Father declares that it was He who was
offended in the transgression, and it was man who offended.
Man, by disobeying, "sins / Against the high Supremacy of
Heav'n, / Affecting God-head" (III.204-6). Consequently, someone who is not only willing, but also able, must act as Mediator.

> He with his whole posterity must die,
> Die hee or Justice must; unless for him
> Some other able, and as willing, pay
> The rigid satisfaction, death for death.
> (III.209-12)

Milton's use of the verb "able" here gives the line an important theological meaning. If the passage had read, "unless for
him / Some other, and as willing, pay," we could conclude that

the Father would be content with anyone who would be willing to undertake the task. But by using the verb "able," the Father is actually limiting the office to one who must be apt, suitable, or fit for the purpose. This meaning is further strengthened by the argument of Book III, which reads: "Man hath offended the Majesty of God by aspiring to Godhead, and therefore with all his Progeny devoted to death must die, unless some one can be found sufficient to answer for his offense, and undergo his Punishment." The Son then offers himself, and the Father cries, "O thou in Heav'n and Earth the only peace / Found out for mankind under wrath, O thou / My sole complacence" (III.274-76), and proceeds to tell the Son that "thir [human] Nature also to thy [divine] Nature join" (III.282). In Milton's scheme, the suitability of Christ for the office of Mediator arises not so much from the God-man/man-God theology of Augustine but from the divine-human/human-divine aspect. This aspect of Augustine's teaching interested Milton for his purpose; and although the two aspects may be similar, there is a shade of difference for Milton. That the Mediator was divine and human makes him the suitable one for mediation, but that he was divine does not necessarily make him equal in a trinitarian sense to the Father.[36] In this Christological sense, Milton departs from Augustine's teaching; yet, in his concept of Mediation, along with the suitability of the divine-human person for the function of Redemption and the offices of Mediation, Milton is Augustinian.

Concerning the mediatorial office, Augustine teaches that the sin of Adam involved all mankind; and, in order that all mankind might obtain salvation,[37] Christ, in virtue of his God-man status, freely performed all that was required for reconciliation with God[38] (John xv.9: "As the Father hath loved me, so have I loved you"). Milton proceeds to define this as "the office by virtue of which He willingly performed, and still performs all those things through which peace with God and eternal salvation for the human race are attained."[39] In the epic, we read: "sending thee / Man's Friend, his Mediator, his design'd / Both Ransom and Redeemer voluntary" (X.59-61).

Augustine attributes to the Mediator the threefold function of prophet, priest, and king.[40] Of the office of prophet, Milton says, "His prophetic function is to educate his church in heavenly truth and to teach the whole will of his Father."[41] The word "prophet" is etymologically derived from the Greek verb προφημι, to say beforehand, to foretell (Hebrew, רֹאֶה, vates, seer); but in a wider sense, it signifies a teacher (magister, διδάσκαλος ; Hebrew, נָבִיא , speaker, orator). The word, when applied to Christ and the Redemption, has always carried with it the twofold meaning of its etymology. For Augustine, to say that Christ exercised the office or function of a prophet is equivalent to saying that he possessed in the highest degree the gift of prophecy and the vocation of a teacher with the highest wisdom and was, consequently, the bearer of truth (John i.16-18: "Grace and truth came by Christ Jesus ... the only begotten Son, which is in the bosom of the Father, he hath declared him"; and iv.25: "Christ, when he is come, he will tell us all things"). Milton says: "His prophetical function consists in two parts: one external and one internal. The first is the revelation of truth, the second the illumination of the mind."[42] He speaks of Christ as "consiliarius" and "Dei sapientia," which appears in the epic as "My word, my wisdom, and effectual might" (III.170), and again, "All hast thou spok'n as my thoughts are, all / As my Eternal purpose hath decreed" (III.171-72).

But the application of the prophetical-teaching office of Christ is not found in *Paradise Lost*, simply because Christ's work as prophet has no function in the epic. There are innumer- prophet Moses, as a type of Christ, prefigures the Mediator, "whose high Office now / Moses in figure bears, to introduce / One greater" (XII.240-42); so does Joshua, "whom the Gentiles Jesus call, / His Name and Office bearing" (XII.310-11). We see Michael, Christ's delegate, as "Prophet of glad tidings, finisher / Of utmost hope" (XII.375-76); and where Christ is to be the fulfillment of prophecy: "That of the Royal Stock / Of David (so I name this King) shall rise / A Son, the Woman's seed to thee foretold" (XII.325-27). As a matter of fact, most of Books XI and XII are prophecy. But it is not until we come to *Paradise Regained* that we come to an application of the prophetical-teaching office on the part of Christ. In an epic where man is the hero, the active life of Christ cannot be too much in evidence. In *Paradise Lost*, Milton's interest is man, and the realization of man's destiny comes through prophecy. Man's salvation, and Christ as a means to it, is revealed through prophecy. In *Para-*

dise Regained, where Christ is central, he is not only the fulfillment of prophecy, but also the last and greatest of the prophets,
who performs all the functions of the office and acts in accordance with what has been predicted of him.

Concerning the priesthood of Christ, Milton says: "The
priestly function is that in accordance with which Christ offered
himself to God the Father as a sacrifice for sinners, and has
always made, and still continues to make intercession for us."[43]
The actual ordination of Christ to the priesthood took place at
the moment of the Incarnation. This is deduced from the fact
that the generation of the Son was for the purpose of redeeming
mankind and for the appeasement of God's anger; and since this
could be done only through the Son's actually sacrificing himself, then the role of sacrificial priest began at his generation.
Milton observes that the Bible gives absolutely clear and unam-
biguous reasons why Christ must have been a man, and the Pauline evidence that he cites for this miraculous incarnation is that
Christ "should be a merciful and faithful high priest" (Heb.
ii.14), and that in Christ "we have not a high priest that cannot
be touched with a feeling of our weaknesses" (Heb. iv.15).[44] The
aim for Christ's miraculous conception was to evade the pollution of Adam's sin, and only "such a high priest was fitting for
us, holy, spotless, separate from sinners" (Heb. vii.26).[45]

Yet, since the definition states that Christ "has always made
... intercession for us," and since Milton frequently alludes to
the eternity of Christ's priesthood, the question of priesthood in
an unfallen world immediately comes to mind. Although Augustine and Milton work with the traditional teaching that Christ
was ordained for sinful man, both do, even if by implication,
give some consideration to the alternative that Christ would
have come into the world even if Adam and Eve had not fallen.
From Milton's adoption of the Pauline theory of the primacy of
Christ;[46] from his exegesis of the opening lines of the Joannine
gospel narrative where he says, "Whatever certain modern scholars may say to the contrary, it is certain that the Son existed in
the beginning, under the title of the Word or Logos, that he was
the first of created things, and that through him all other things,
both in heaven and earth, were afterwards made";[47] from his
assertion that, like his prophetic function which began at the
beginning of the world, so, too, in his priestly function "he was

given and sacrificed from the beginning of the world even for those to whom he was not known and believed only in God the Father"[48]—from these examples, we can presume that Milton felt that Christ would have come into the world as eternal high priest if Adam had not fallen. He says that "Christ's kingdom ...is like his priesthood, eternal";[49] and in discussing the meaning of eternity, Milton says "nothing can properly be called eternal unless it has no beginning and no end."[50] Christ's priesthood, then, regardless of his generation, has no beginning and no end. Therefore, the firstborn of all creation offered himself as sacrificing priest even when unfallen man lived in his unfallen world—indeed, even before.

This priesthood, of course, would be in the form of adoration, the formal element of sacrifice, and not of expiation, the secondary element of sacrifice. It must be remembered that adoration is the formal element of every sacrifice, i.e., that which essentially constituted it a sacrifice in the strict sense of the term. Expiation does not enter into the essence of sacrifice but is merely a secondary factor, because it is conditioned by the accidental fact of sin. Since thanksgiving and supplication, when addressed to the Almighty, invariably and necessarily partake of the nature of absolute worship, sacrifices offered up for these two purposes have no relation to sin. The case is different with expiatory sacrifices. While sin has neither abolished nor debased (but, rather, reinforced) the main purpose of adoration (namely, thanksgiving and supplication), it has added a new object which, though in itself secondary, has become inseparable from the notion of sacrifice in consequence of the Fall. This is discussed with special sensitivity by Augustine in *De Civitate Dei*, X.5-6. Christ's coming, then, as priest, if there had been no Fall of Man, would be solely in the sacrificial role of adoration, the adoring priest.

But in the present economy of things, whereby Adam and Eve did fall and are redeemed, Christ, at his Incarnation, came in the sacrificial role of propitiation, the suffering priest. It is this propitiatory aspect of sacrifice that emphasizes the offering of a victim and some symbolic act, such as bloodletting or slaying. By custom and language, the word sacrifice has come to be used as almost synonymous with slaying or mactation, but it should be noticed that in many sacrifices there is no such action present.

Not even all of the Jewish sacrifices were propitiatory, although the sense of guilt seems rarely to be altogether absent from them. The imagery of a suffering Christ pacifying a cruel and angry God is perhaps a perversion of this expiatory aspect of sacrifice which found its way down into the seventeenth century and into Milton's thought. That Milton understood this distinction in the concept of sacrifice is apparent when he discusses the fact that Christ has always made intercession for man by "inciting and urging us, in other words, to address God as our Father through faith. This, of course, is easily distinguishable from the priestly function of importuning God, by virtue of which Christ intercedes for us";[51] the inciting of mankind to "address God ...through faith" is the formal element of sacrifice, and the "importuning God" is the secondary element. In an unfallen world, Christ as priest would most likely have acted as model or example for Adam on how to adore, teaching Adam and Eve through adoration how to grow in sanctity and obedience, thereby preparing them for the eventual transferral into heaven which was their destiny from the beginning had they obeyed (see *PL* VII.154-61).

Milton's whole treatment of Christ as priest in *Christian Doctrine* and in the two epics of paradise is generally from the expiatory and propitiatory point of view of sacrifice, and rightfully so, for Milton is concerned with the present order of things, a fallen world. So, too, then, Christ as priest, in virtue of the eternity of his priesthood, "still continues to make intercession for us" as long as there is occasion for him to carry out the function of a mediator.[52] It seems here that an end is assigned to Christ's priestly function, that is, when there is nothing or no one to mediate for any longer. But Milton is careful in referring to Christ's kingdom of glory, where, granted, the priestly function of Mediator may come to an end but the priesthood of Christ, which is identified with the kingdom of glory and the church, will not.[53] This fact makes all the more interesting and all the more accurate Howard Schultz's observation that the storm-tower sequence in *Paradise Regained* represents the continuation of Christ's suffering and triumph in the church throughout history.[54] And, as Barbara Lewalski observes: "The storm imagery suggests the Church subject to persecution by Satan and the world, and also suggests the violence and terror of the Last Day.

... Similarly, the glorious dawn following after the storm represents the millennial reign of Christ and his saints, the tower scene suggests the last grand battle wherein Christ will overthrow Satan, and the angelic banquet symbolizes the church's communion which celebrates Christ's priestly sacrifice and which itself prefigures the 'marriage supper of the Lamb'.''[55] Both scholars here are considering Christ's priesthood as a function that continues now and will continue forever. It is not unusual to find Milton speaking in one breath of the eternity of Christ's priesthood—that is, that it had no beginning and will have no end—and then, in another, of the priesthood as beginning with the Incarnation and ending when the mediatorial mission is fulfilled. Augustine and many of the Fathers did the same, and, by so doing, presumed that their readers understood the twofold purpose of every sacrifice: that of adoration, which is independent of sin and which was Christ's as adoring priest; and that of expiation, which concerns a fallen world and which was Christ's as redeeming priest.

After defining Christ's priesthood, Milton goes on to discuss in closer detail its specific nature—the humiliation and the exaltation of Christ. The humiliation is that whereby, as God-man, Christ "submitted himself voluntarily, both in life and in death, to the Divine Justice, in order to suffer all the things which were necessary for our redemption."[56] From the outset Milton asserts that Christ submitted himself as true God-man, that is, that he suffered both in his human nature and his divine nature. He says: "Of course, the fact that Christ became a sacrifice both in his divine and in his human nature is questioned by no one. It is, moreover, necessary for the whole of a sacrifice to be killed. So it follows that Christ, the sacrificial lamb, was totally killed."[57] However, despite the fact that Christ's divine nature partook of the sacrifice, Milton says: "A large number of biblical texts make it clear that it was *especially* in his human nature that he offered himself" (italics mine).[58]

Augustine is cautious in this area when he states that the Divine Logos did indeed suffer, but only according to his passible manhood. The difference in the two thinkers, though it be slight, goes back to their teaching on the Trinity and the hypostatic union. Augustine, whose Trinitarian doctrine teaches that Christ is of the same essence as God the Father (three persons in the Trinity but not three essences), cannot bring himself to teach that Christ suffered fully in his two natures, since this would imply that the Trinity (God the Father) was sacrificed.[59] Milton, on the other hand, who goes through such pains in proving that the Son is a complete, distinct, and separate essence from the Father (see the whole of Chapter V in *Christian Doctrine*), and who teaches that Christ is subordinate to the Father in the Trinitarian hierarchy and the Son is divine only by allotment (an allotment commensurate with the mission involved), maintains that Christ suffered fully in his divine as well as in his human nature. So, too, the divine nature succumbed to death, which, of course, follows from the poet's mortalism theory.[60] (This erratic teaching again acts as a stumbling block for the poet. Here he has difficulty reconciling with this theory Christ's statement to the good thief that "today you will be with me in paradise," and the explanation of the text he advances is fumbled.)

In any case, the important thing is that Augustine insists that the priesthood and sacrifice, although the Divine Logos suffered, were in Christ's passible manhood; and Milton insists that, although both natures suffered, it was especially in Christ's humanity that the priesthood and sacrifice took place. To go beyond this in establishing any doctrinal similarities or any Miltonic indebtedness to Augustine is impossible, in part because of the enormous difference in their Trinitarian teaching, and moreso because neither thinker addresses himself with much conviction to some of the problems that their teachings here provoke. In what sense Christ offered and accepted simultaneously the sacrifice of the Cross, and wherein precisely did the *actio sacrificia* of Christ's bloody sacrifice consist, are not treated in any way by Milton and are treated only half-heartedly and superficially by Augustine. The important thing here is the similarity of the two thinkers in the broad, general, and immensely important teaching that the priesthood rested mainly in the humanity of Christ, a teaching that Milton found invaluable for his dramatic purpose in *Paradise Regained*.

The satisfaction of Christ means that "Christ fully satisfied Divine Justice by fulfilling the law and paying the just price on behalf of all men."[61] Concerning Christ's satisfaction, Milton, like Augustine, is very definite about the events here: there was plainly a substitute of one person for another, there was a true

bloody sacrifice, and the debt was fully paid. Christ offered the
sacrifice and was the victim being offered; he was high priest
and victim. After citing evidence from Paul that the sacrifice was
a true one, Milton asserts that "those who maintain that Christ
sought death not in our place and for the sake of redemption,
but only for our good and in order to set an example, try in vain
to evade the evidence of these texts."[62]

By using the expression "paying the just price"[63] in his definition of satisfaction, Milton evokes the "ransom theory" of Redemption which was so prevalent among Church Fathers, particularly Augustine. According to this view, the death and
resurrection of Christ represent some kind of transaction with,
or deception of and conquest over, the devil. The view was crit-
icized by Anselm, held by Augustine, received dogmatic status
in the Calvinist churches, and had been assumed by most Protestants and Catholics up to the time of Milton. The view
teaches essentially that the devil, having successfully caused
Adam to sin, had a just right of possession over him and his
offspring, for he gained them and kept them in his power by fair
means, working upon their minds and hearts through persuasion and evoking their free consent. But the devil, who held men
justly, was also overcome justly. He had rights over Adam and
over those men who consented to the temptations and were thus
held guilty before God; but he did not have rights over the
Second Adam, who lived without concupiscence and who was
without Original Sin.[64]

Two features of this theory have often given offense: the suggestion that the devil has rights, and the notion of a ransom
paid to the devil. Concerning the devil's having rights, Augustine ably discusses this in *De Ordine*, where, within the context
of a larger discussion on the providential ordering of the world,
he demonstrates that through sanctifying grace Adam and Eve
before their fall were in a higher spiritual realm than the fallen
angels, but with their transgression they were relegated to a
lower realm in the hierarchical scale than Satan.[65] Concerning
ransom or price (Matt. xx.28: "A ransom for many"; and I Cor.
vi.20: "bought with a price"), Augustine often uses the patristic
imagery of a tricking of the devil, with the humanity of Christ
functioning like the bait in a mousetrap (*esca in muscipula*); but
this is used only to highlight two important parallels: there is a

deliverance from captivity, and it takes place according to the standards of justice or right governing the relationship between two parties. What happened, however, was an overstepping of the bounds of one party. The devil, through an excess of zeal, exercises his rights in an improper way; and he forfeits his rights over those who adhere in Christ.[66]

Increasingly, the ransom theory was supplemented by another theme in Augustine's works, that of sacrifice (Heb. x.12: "he had offered one sacrifice for sins for ever"). Christ was called the righteous priest who offered his own unblemished life to God in behalf of mankind, from whom he received his humanity. The function of this sacrifice was said to be to reconcile men to God, to reunite them with him; and it is accomplished by Christ in such a way that, while he remains one with God to whom the offering is made, he is both offerer and offering.[67] Consequently, the "satisfaction theory," which was to become fully developed in Anselm, supplements the "ransom theory" in Augustine's theology of Redemption; and the co-existence of the two theories suggests the two aspects of sacrifice. Sacrifice is treated by Augustine as an inward act of total devotion of mind, heart, and strength; it is not confined to the death of Christ but pertains to his whole human activity. Ransom, on the other hand, has to do solely with Christ's suffering—a death freely offered with the consequence that men are liberated from their bondage to evil.

How much Milton was aware of these theories we do not know from *Christian Doctrine*, and it really does not much matter. What does matter is the fact that the theory had so infiltrated Christian thought right down to Milton's time that his whole discussion of atonement, redemption, and satisfaction is couched in ransom imagery. Such passages from the epic as: "So only can high Justice rest appaid" (XII.401); "Obedience to the Law of God, impos'd / On penalty of death" (XII.397–98); and "Die hee or Justice must; unless for him / Some other able, and as willing, pay / The rigid satisfaction" (III.210–12), read as if they emerge solely from the ransom theory. Also, the rigid and strict justice business (observed by many critics) in an epic that purports to justify the ways of a merciful God to man, indeed the very portrayal of God as strict judge and dull dictator, reflect this background which is not necessarily only Puritan but also Augustinian. When we realize that the theory would not have been thought of by Milton as an amicable transaction nor a deception on God's part but actually an open confrontation with the forces of evil, we can understand why the poet was so attracted to it for his dramatic purpose. One of the main features of the ransom theory that made it worthwhile for Milton's consideration is that it is firmly set within earthly life, more in keeping with the gospel narratives which present it as a drama played out between finite agents—the forces of evil, the human Christ, the Adam who stands between them—with tangible problems of religion and obedience, with bids being made, and with the stakes being eternal life and death. This is unlike the view of Anselm and his successors, which locates the focus of redemption in the hidden depths of God and even in the intra-Trinitarian relations.[68] Indeed, the ransom theory contributed to the idea of conflict so integral to and so necessarily a part of epic decorum.

Another feature of the satisfaction of Christ's priesthood is that it was "on behalf of all men" (Rom. v.18: "The free gift came upon all men"). Through Adam's sin, death came into the world; and the Second Adam repaired the evil by a death in which we all mystically share. This does not mean, however, that without further ado all are destined for heaven. Though the Redemption through Christ's priesthood is objective, there is nothing mechanical about it. Augustine insists that the change of status required for man to pass from his natural state, disordered by sin, into one of sonship with Christ was beyond his power; therefore, the redemptive act of Christ is to that extent independent of human meriting. But in the very redemptive act, Christ acted as the Head of the human race. Therefore, the will to share as a member with the Head, the will to belong to him freely, the will to do good works, is needed for the Redemption to be efficacious (Tit. ii.14: "Who gave himself for us, that he might redeem us from all iniquity, and purify unto himself a peculiar people, zealous of good works"; and Matt. xxiii.37: "O Jerusalem...how often would I have gathered thy children together...and ye would not"). That all men died in Adam and that all men, of necessity, are included in Christ's redeeming blood is probably the most repeated teaching in *Christian Doctrine*, and certainly one of the principal doctrines underlying the theology of *Paradise Lost* and *Paradise Regained*.

In the treatise, Milton explicitly refutes any teaching that Christ died for the elect. He says: "Sufficient grace is imparted to all men. So it must follow that Christ has made satisfaction for all men to a sufficient extent and efficaciously enough to meet the requirements of God's plan and will. For without that absolutely full satisfaction even the smallest measure of grace could not possibly have been imparted to all."[69] He asserts that the sacrifice "was not only sufficient in itself but also effectual," and, in typically Miltonic fashion, the efficacy of the sacrifice "depends upon the faith of man. If there is not enough faith to make the satisfaction effectual, then it does not mean that the satisfaction was not given effectually, but simply that it was not accepted." Milton here establishes a distinction between "to redeem" and "to purify," and, in so doing, he avoids any Lutheran teaching that man is saved by faith alone. He says: "Christ has redeemed all transgressors but he purifies only those who are eager to do good works, in other words, believers. For without belief no works are good. All are redeemed, even those who are ignorant of it, or who are still opposed to Christ. . . . But no one is purified except through faith, and unless he is willing; the Bible frequently states this."[70] Furthermore, he says: "Faith has its own works, which may be different from the works of the law. We are justified, then, by faith, but a living faith, not a dead one, and the only living faith is a faith which acts, James ii, 17, 20, 26. So we are justified by faith without the works of the law, but not without the works of faith; for a true and living faith cannot exist without works, though these may be different from the works of the written law."[71] Consequently, the satisfaction of Christ's priesthood, embracing all men (not fallen angels), is universal. As Augustine observed, "The blood of thy Lord is given for thee, if thou wilt; if thou wilt not, it is not given for thee."[72] Milton teaches that its efficacy depends upon man himself.

Milton defines the mediatorial office of king as that whereby Christ, "having been made a king by God the Father, rules and preserves, principally by internal law and spiritual power, the Church which he has bought for himself, and conquers and crushes his enemies."[73] The traditional concept that Christ is set at the right hand of the Father, in the heavenly places, above all principality and power, virtue, and dominion, with all things subject to him,[74] appears in the epic:

> Here shalt thou sit incarnate, here shalt Reign
> Both God and Man, Son both of God and Man,
> Anointed universal King; all Power
> I give thee, reign for ever, and assume
> Thy merits; under thee as Head Supreme
> Thrones, Princedoms, Powers, Dominions I reduce:
> All knees to thee shall bow, of them that bide
> In Heaven, or Earth, and under Earth in Hell;
> (III.315–22)

The importance of the kingship of Christ is that he is made head over all the Church which he founded[75] (Luke i.32: "The Lord God shall give unto him the throne of his father David: and he shall reign over the house of Jacob; and of his kingdom there shall be no end"; and Col. i.18: "And he is the head of the body, the Church"). Milton terms this "acquisitam ab se ecclesiam," and in the poem, "he shall ascend / The Throne hereditary, and bound his Reign / With earth's wide bounds, his glory with the Heav'ns" (XII.369–71). Contrary to what had been expected, his kingdom is not of this world, but is a kingdom of the spirit, and the power which he exercises is spiritual only[76] (John xviii.36: "My kingdom is not of this world"). Milton, who speaks of the kingdom of grace and the kingdom of glory, teaches the spirituality of Christ's kingdom when he says: "This makes it apparent how superior Christ's kingdom is to all others. It also makes apparent its divine nature, because he rules not only the body, as a civil magistrate does, but above all he rules the mind and the conscience. He does this, moreover, not by force or by physical weapons, but by those things which, in the opinion of the world, are the weakest of all. Therefore external force should never be used in Christ's kingdom, the Church."[77]

This concept of the spiritual kingdom of Christ, and the Church as the kingdom of Christ, appears again and again in Milton's discussion *De Ecclesia Visibili* and in the four closing chapters of Book I of *Christian Doctrine*, where it is treated as a study separate from the Redemption. But the spiritual kingdom of Christ and the spiritual principles upon which his Church rests are very significantly the means by which Adam and Eve "shalt possess / A paradise within" of far more happiness. When Gabriel sums up for Adam the nature of good conduct, he is actually advising him to embrace the spiritual principles which underlie Christ's spiritual kingdom, the Church, and which will eventually defeat Satan in *Paradise Regained,* where again we see a fuller application of this office. He tells Adam to embrace virtue, patience, temperance, and love, "By name to come call'd Charity, the soul / Of all the rest: then wilt thou not be loath / To leave this Paradise" (XII.584-86). Concerning the conflict to come between Christ and Satan, Michael says, "Dream not of thir fight, / As of a Duel, or the local wounds / Of head or heel" (XII.386-88), for these worldly-wise and worldly-strong tactics will no longer bring victory. Now it is good works and the things of the spirit that will triumph "by fulfilling that which thou didst want, / Obedience to the Law of God" (XII.396-97). Christ's victory over Satan will come through virtue and love, all those virtues we see at work in *Paradise Regained,* and God will be appeased through Christ in the same fashion: "The Law of God exact he shall fulfil / Both by obedience and by love, though love / Alone fulfil the Law" (XII.402-4). Participation in the spiritual kingdom of Christ will be "by small / Accomplishing great things, by things deem'd weak / Subverting worldly strong, and worldly wise / By simply meek" (XII.566-69). Adam, then, "Greatly instructed" and "Greatly in peace of thought," concludes that the only victory is that of the spirit, "that to obey is best, / And love with fear the only God, to walk / As in his presence" (XII.561-63), and the poem ends on the dominant note of humility.

If the epic seems to manifest an almost limited treatment of Christ's three offices, it is because Milton is keeping within the demands of the subject matter. Paradise is lost. Man lost it, and it must be regained for man. Consequently, the offices and functions of Christ are introduced only in relationship to man and man's regaining Paradise. If Milton had incorporated into the epic all the implications of Christ's threefold office and examples of actual application from his external life, *Paradise Lost* would have taken upon itself the additional subject matter of a life of Christ, and the epic would have been doubled in length.

But, as it stands, the offices are given the amount of treatment proportionate to the demands of the epic, and in such a way that man will benefit by it. Christ, the prophet-teacher, is the fulfillment of all the prophecies which Adam can expect with great anticipation, for it is man's seed that will redeem. Christ, the priest, is the sacrificial lamb, whose sacrificial act will adequately unite man with God again. Christ, the king, is the founder of the Church whose spiritual and divine principles are the means whereby man will find salvation; indeed, as we have seen in Milton's soteriology, the kingship office is given secondary place to the redemptive office for the sake of man. The three offices, then, are seen only in their relationship to man, which obviously suited Milton's purpose. To go beyond this would be to go beyond the scope of the epic.

Milton's handling of the three offices accounts in no small way for his portrayal of Christ in the epic. Our first contact with the Son in *Paradise Lost* is in the famous "council in Heaven" scene of Book III. It contains what is probably the most theological of all the dialogues that Milton ever wrote; and the risks he takes are many, not only because theological theorizing in verse is risky business, but also because immediately the reader discerns a contrast between God—the anthropomorphic, omnipotent Father—and his Son, who is not yet human but whose speech already reveals attractive human qualities. The dramatic contrasts and their dramatic significance, particularly in the hell of Books I and II and the heaven of Book III, have been stressed by B. Rajan, Ernest Schanzer, Irene Samuel, J. B. Broadbent, and others.[78] But here we have a contrast within Book III between the Father and Son; and in the dramatic situation, the Son emerges as far more attractive than the Father. Merritt Y. Hughes has rightly observed that, by abandoning the debate between Justice and Mercy (which Milton "had sketched at some length, probably earlier than 1640, in the third of his four 'outlines for tragedy' on the theme of *Paradise Lost* in the Trinity College Manuscript"),[79] the poet has found a way of establishing a dialogue between distinct persons. However reluctant we may be to accept John Peter's position that from the dialogue the reader is immediately confronted with an unfavorable first impression of God and a far more successful first impression of the Son,[80] we cannot ignore the fact that the Son here is more humane and self-sacrificing, that he responds in favor of mercy rather than justice, and that, as a consequence, he is far more human than divine. It is this humanity that will be dramatically delineated in greater depth in *Paradise Regained*. The worldly qualities of the three redemptive offices, which are often alluded to in the dialogue and which the Son will exercise on his mission, are far more attractive than the abstract attributes which are the Father's and which characterize his speech.[81]

Throughout the epic, we never lose sight of the reason for the existence of Christ, Mediator and Redeemer; and the three offices which are an integral part of his mission are always implicit in the early books, and are explicitly delineated in Books XI and XII. This emphasis on the humanity of Christ has been a source of distress for some readers, particularly for those who hug closely the terms orthodox and unorthodox. But the total humanity of Christ is well established in the Christian tradition, and Milton's Christ, particularly in Book III and throughout the epic, is much in conformity with Augustinian teaching. This is not to say that Milton's subordinationist view[82]—that the Son is inferior to the Father—is Augustinian; it is merely to assert that Milton's emphasis on the humanity of Christ is well established in Augustine. And if Milton's Christ acts like a true representative of humanity and manifests all the human qualities of a full man, it is simply because he is just that—as Augustine so convincingly taught. The human, worldly, manly qualities of epic figures are, of course, part of epic decorum. But they are also traceable to the examples of Scriptural types of Christ, and still more to the doctrine of Atonement and Redemption and the three offices, and to all the traditional imagery associated with the offices.

The insistence by some critics on the vast differences that exist between the Father and the Son in their speeches and activity seems to me to distort Milton's Trinitarian teaching and to ignore the happenings after Book III. C. A. Patrides makes an excellent case for the unity of the Father and the Son in the epic when he suggests that "the distinction between the Father and the Son in *Paradise Lost* appears only in their verbal exchanges, while as soon as the 'dialogues' are terminated, and particularly when we encounter the Godhead in action beyond the confines of heaven, the distinction between the two persons is arrested abruptly."[83] God's prophetic summary in Book III is necessarily theological, but we must beware of considering these utterances in total isolation, thereby labeling him a dull dictator. We hear what God has to say and we hear what the Son has to say, and the whole divine interchange is a joint activity of Father and Son. As Harry Blamires has observed, you "cannot, unless you are a polytheist (and Milton certainly was not), have one God who punishes and another who saves. If justice and mercy, authority and compassion, meet and mingle in the interchange of dialogue between Father and Son, they do so in the unity of a single Godhead."[84] Within the context of *Paradise Lost*, Milton has retained his Trinitarian orthodoxy, subordinationist though it may be. God the Son is God, too, and outside "the confines of heaven," the activity of the Deity is an intertwined pattern of action which reveals to us the nature of God. In other words, in Book III two sides of the same character are being revealed. In the remainder of the epic, the more human side, the Son, who is still God, dominates the action.

The Qualities of Redemption

Milton's three principal concepts of redemption, humiliation, and exaltation are characteristic of traditional Augustinian teaching. That Christ, sent by God, freely shed his blood for the sins of man is the very essence of Augustinian teaching on Redemption.[85] Milton says, "Redemption is the act by which Christ, sent in the fulness of time, redeemed all believers at the price of his own blood, which he paid voluntarily in accordance with the eternal plan and grace of God the Father."[86] In the poem we read:

> nor can this be,
> But by fulfilling that which thou didst want,
> Obedience to the Law of God, impos'd
> On penalty of death, and suffering death,
> The penalty to thy transgression due,
> And due to theirs which out of thine will grow:
> So only can high Justice rest appaid.
> The Law of God exact he shall fulfil

> Both by obedience and by love, though love
> Alone fulfil the Law, thy punishment
> He shall endure by coming in the Flesh
> To a reproachful life and cursed death,
> Proclaiming Life to all who shall believe
> In his redemption.
>
> (XII.395–408)

Concerning the humiliation of Christ, Augustine teaches that he was wounded for our iniquities; he was bruised for our sins,[87] and by his bruises we were healed, and God laid on him the iniquity of us all[88] (Phil. ii.6–8: "He humbled himself, and became obedient unto death, even the death of the cross"). Milton says the humiliation of Christ is that state in which "the God-man submitted himself voluntarily, both in life and in death, to the divine justice, in order to suffer all the things which were necessary for our redemption."[89] Michael foretells: "He shall live hated, be blasphem'd, / Seiz'd on by force, judg'd, and to death condemn'd / A shameful and accurst" (XII.411–13). But, in turn, he will rise from the dead, ascend into heaven, and sit at the right hand of the Father[90] (Eph. iv.8: "He ascended up on high"; and Matt. xxvi.65: "Sitting on the right hand"), which Milton terms the exaltation. "Christ, having triumphed over death and laid aside the form of a servant, was raised to immortality and to the highest glory of God the Father, for our good, by virtue partly of his own merit and partly of the Father's gift, and rose again, and ascended, and sits at God's right hand."[91] Michael continues his instruction of Adam by explaining the three degrees of exaltation—Resurrexit: "so he dies, / But soon revives, Death over him no power / Shall long usurp" (XII.419–21); ascendit: "Then to the Heav'n of Heav'ns he shall ascend / With victory, triumphing through the air / Over his foes and thine" (XII.451–53); Dextram [sic] Dei sedet: "and resume / His Seat at God's right hand, exalted high / Above all names in Heav'n" (XI.456–58).

In dealing with these three principal concepts of the redemptive work, Milton has treated various aspects of the dogma of the Redemption which modern theologians have termed the "perfection of Christ's redemption." The perfection of Christ's redemption is described as adequate, universal, and superabundant. By adequate is meant that the sacrifice made by Christ is sufficient of itself, by its own intrinsic merit, to counterbalance the evil of sin (Heb. x.14: "For by one offering he hath perfected forever them that are sanctified"; and I John i.7: "The blood of Jesus Christ his Son cleanseth us from all sin"). The infinite dignity of Christ as God-man gave to his actions an infinite value, and when we add to that the natural dignity, the love and obedience, shown in the sacrifice of the passion,[92] the truth of the assertion seems obvious. Milton's thoughts on the adequacy of Christ's redemptive work can be seen as early as when he speaks of the two natures of the Redeemer. In the treatise, he observes that "God would not accept any other sacrifice since any other would have been less worthy." He teaches that Christ performed whatever was requisite to accomplish the Redemption and that a complete reparation was made. Consequently, "the effect of this satisfaction extends to the reconciliation of God the Father with man."[93] For Milton, the adequacy of Christ's redemptive work arises in his teaching on the suitability of Christ as a divine human Mediator. "Thou therefore whom thou only canst redeem" (III.281), because he is both human and divine. Probably the most significant passage in *Paradise Lost* with regard to the adequacy of Christ's work is in Book III, when the Son assures the Father of the success of his future redemptive mission and the satisfaction the Father will receive from it:

> Thou at the sight
> Pleas'd, out of Heaven shalt look down and smile,
> While by thee rais'd I ruin all my Foes,
> Death last, and with his Carcass glut the Grave:
> Then with the multitude of my redeem'd
> Shall enter Heav'n long absent, and return,
> Father, to see thy face, wherein no cloud
> Of anger shall remain, but peace assur'd,
> And reconcilement; wrath shall be no more
> Thenceforth, but in thy presence Joy entire.
> (III.256–65)

And later,

this God-like act
Annuls thy doom, the death thou shouldst have di'd,
In sin for ever lost from life; this act
Shall bruise the head of Satan, crush his strength
Defeating Sin and Death.

(XII.427-31)

The universality of the Redemption objectively coincides with the universality of God's will to save the entire human race. St. Paul emphasizes the universality of God's will to save all men in the words, "Who gave himself Redemption for all" (I Tim. ii.16). Augustine feels that if all men fell in Adam, in virtue of the principle of corporateness and co-inherence, it is the mind of God that all men should rise in Christ.[94] Milton uses the same reasoning in commenting on II Corinthians v.15 when he says, "If this follows, then the converse is also true, if all were dead because Christ died for all, then he died for all who were dead, that is everyone."[95] In the epic, we read: "As in him perish all men, so in thee / As from a second root shall be restor'd / As many as are restor'd, without thee none" (III.287-89). However, this doctrine does not mean that in virtue of Christ's redemptive merits all will be saved automatically. The universality of Christ's redemption is not absolute, but conditional; and the condition is that "he be newborn in Christ."[96] Milton, like Augustine, maintains that Christ died for all men; and the fact that so many human beings are eternally lost does not disprove the universality of the Redemption—it merely proves that they did not comply with the conditions necessary for participating in the redemptive work[97] (John xv.22: "If I had not come and spoken unto them, they had not had sin: but now they have no excuse for their sin").

The aspect of man's freedom to cooperate in the redemptive merits of Christ is an important one and appears often in the treatise. Under the renovation of man, Milton speaks of the Father, who, "out of gratuitous kindness, invites believers to salvation so that those who do not believe are deprived of all excuse."[98] God calls all mankind to salvation—all are called to partake in its benefits—because the ransom Christ paid is of itself sufficient for the redemption of all mankind. But not all comply. For Augustine, those who do are said to be in "Christ

renewed,"⁹⁹ and for Milton, those who do are said to be in
"Christ regenerated."¹⁰⁰ In *Paradise Lost*, the liberty which was
man's before the Fall applies as well after the Fall. The Redemption applies to man if he chooses to renounce himself and live
transplanted in Christ.

> His crime makes guilty all his Sons, thy merit
> Imputed shall absolve them who renounce
> Thir own both righteous and unrighteous deeds,
> And live in thee transplanted, and from thee
> Receive new life.

(III.290-94)

In Book XII, we see that, with Christ and the new inward law,
man is free to be his follower: "From imposition of strict Laws,
to free / Acceptance of large Grace" (304-5). And with the freedom to cooperate in the prophecy of the Holy Spirit, whereby
the Spirit will be sent as a guide to aid man in his choice, "the
Law of Faith / Working through love, upon thir hearts shall
write, / To guide them in all truth" (XII.488-90). Man's choice
and freedom are explicit in the passage "Man shall not quite be
lost, but sav'd who will, / Yet not of will in him, but grace in
me / Freely voutsaf't" (III.173-75); and

> The rest shall hear me call, and oft be warn'd
> Thir sinful state, and to appease betimes
> Th'incensed Deity while offer'd grace
> Invites; for I will clear thir senses dark,
> What may suffice, and soft'n stony hearts
> To pray, repent, and bring obedience due.
> To Prayer, repentance, and obedience due
> Though but endeavor'd with sincere intent,
> Mine ear shall not be slow, mine eye not shut.

(III.185-93)

Those who refuse, "They who neglect and scorn, shall never
taste; / But hard be hard'n'd, blind be blinded more, / That they
may stumble on, and deeper fall" (III.199-201).

Finally, Christ's redemptive merits were superabundant, an aspect which is derived from Paul's "Where sin abounded, grace did more abound" (Rom. v.20). This inference is demanded by all the rules of theological logic. It is the teaching of both Augustine and Milton that no one but a God-man was able to give adequate satisfaction for the sin of mankind, because not only was it a man who offended, but it was God who was infinitely offended. Consequently, each and every redemptive action performed by this man who was divine is by its very nature infinitely meritorious. So, if the intrinsic worth was actually infinite, then Christ's redemptive act was superabundantly meritorious—that is to say, far in excess of the sins of a human for which it was made.[101] This is a logical result of an act performed by a man who was divine. In the treatise, Milton is merely expounding the doctrine of Paul and Augustine when he speaks of the restoration as an act whereby man, "freed from sin and death by God the Father through Jesus Christ, is raised to a far more excellent state of grace and glory than from which he fell,"[102] and this is repeated in the epic.

Adam's joy in the "felix culpa" is certainly not for the sin committed, but for the superabundant merit derived from the act of Redemption. The remarkable passage in Book XII (469-78) is simply re-echoing the superabundant worth of Christ's redemption. The paradox is excellent for Milton's dramatic purpose, but over and above this, it is theologically sound. Unless we understand the subtlety of the doctrine as Milton understood it, we might easily come to a misunderstanding of the paradox involved. If man had never fallen, and if—as is maintained in Scotistic theology discussed earlier in this chapter on the problem of soteriology—God had deigned to assume the impassible nature of sinless humanity in order to dwell with mankind in a created form and live as a creature in the world created for himself, thereby completing and crowning the work of creation, this would have been a work of infinite love altogether beyond the comprehension of mere created intelligence. But this did not happen. That God took upon himself our passible nature and actually suffered, and exhausted all manner of suffering, mental and corporal, not only in spite of Adam's sin, but in order to redeem Adam and mankind for his sin, and to make us adopted children of God—this stupendous revelation of God's love it is that makes the Christian tradition exult, "O felix culpa."

As far as forgiveness of sin is concerned, God could have absolved man from it without taking our passible nature. Of this we can be certain from the fact that he is "ipse se subsistens." It is in the mercifulness of this remedial character of the Incarnation occasioned by Adam's fall that the tradition rejoices, "O felix culpa." No praise of the sin of Adam is implied in this doctrine; sin is accepted as a consequence of his freedom. Its meaning is that Divine Wisdom knows how to draw good out of evil. The Fall becomes fortunate, post factum, because of the Incarnation, and thus creates something of a paradox. Though heartbroken with sorrow for his sin, Adam's joy is even greater, or, at least, more intense, at the Divine forgiveness. That is how Augustine saw the happy fault. The grief for Adam's sin is there; but now the rejoicing is that God, who had no part in the sin, took occasion from it more wondrously to manifest his mercy, power, and wisdom. In *Paradise Lost*, the elements of the doctrine are effectively incorporated in the last three books.[103] In Book X, we see Adam's remorse in the famous lament which begins with "O miserable of happy! is this the end / Of this new glorious World, and mee so late / The Glory of that Glory" (720-22) and continues to line 844. In Book XI, we have the important passage which in no way praises the sin of Adam that occasions the good to come from it, "but let him boast / His knowledge of Good lost, and Evil got, / Happier, had it suffic'd him to have known / Good by itself, and Evil not at all" (86-89). And, finally, in Book XII, post factum, we have the magnificent manifestation of God's goodness and mercy:

> O goodness infinite, goodness immense!
> That all this good of evil shall produce,
> And evil turn to good; more wonderful
> Than that which by creation first brought forth
> Light out of darkness! full of doubt I stand,
> Whether I should repent me now of sin
> By mee done and occasion'd, or rejoice
> Much more, that much more good thereof shall spring,
> To God more glory, more good will to Men
> From God, and over wrath grace shall abound.
>
> (469-78)

Milton's doctrine is a logical outcome of his teaching on Original Sin. Even sinful man still retained an intellect which could know good, a will that could judge right from wrong, and a freedom whereby he could choose between right and wrong. This element of choice, ever present in Milton's thought, is at the heart of his doctrine of the Redemption, which teaches that man *can* save himself through the merits of Christ. The freedom which Milton insists upon is the pattern of freedom which dominates the whole epic. Man was free to fall; so, too, he is free to choose salvation. The first man chose sin, and the sin was his own; now salvation is his, if he so chooses. But the Augustinian perception of overwhelming divine love is still apparent. Salvation is actually the work of divine love; and this divine love (grace) acts before, above, and beyond man's initiative—it is over and above man's powers, yet it presses in on him, seeking his cooperation. Consequently, man is the very center of Milton's doctrine of Redemption. Milton's introduction of the three offices of Christ certainly confirms the poet's faith in the divinity of Christ. The objection that Milton's Christ is too human, too much man, is not a valid one when we consider that the offices carry with them such divine characteristics. The offices are just another way of elevating man's humanity to the status of divinity. In the epic, however, the three offices are used primarily for the purpose of instructing and revealing to man the way to truth and salvation. Never does Milton lose sight of what he obviously considered the most important aspect of the plan of salvation— man, God's esteem for man, God's unmerited favor toward man.

Notes

Chapter 1

1. Isabel MacCaffrey, *"Paradise Lost" as Myth* (Cambridge, Mass.: Harvard University Press, 1959), p. 25.
2. Burton O. Kurth, *Milton and Christian Heroism* (Hamden, Conn.: Anchor Books, 1966), p. 109.
3. Nigel Abercrombie, *Saint Augustine and French Classical Thought* (Oxford: The Clarendon Press, 1938). p. 6.
4. Arthur Barker, "Milton's Schoolmasters," *Modern Language Review* 32 (1937):521.
5. A. F. Leach, "Milton as Schoolboy and Schoolmaster," *Proceedings of the British Academy* 3 (1908).
6. Joseph H. Lupton, *Life of Dean Colet* (London: George Bell & Sons, 1909), p. 57. Foster Watson, in his study on the curriculum of the English grammar schools to 1660, sees Charles Hoole's *New Discovery of the Old Art of Teaching School* as clearly representative of the period. Hoole lists the most complete account of the period between 1600 and 1660 and suggests "that children should buy copies of Gerard's *Meditations*, Thomas à Kempis's *Imitation*, and S. Augustine's *Soliloquies* and *Meditations*." Hoole maintains that the children can advantage themselves by perusal of these works available both in English and Latin, and should "continually bear them about in their pockets to read in their spare time." *English Grammar Schools to 1660: Their curriculum and practice* (Cambridge: University Press, 1908), p. 304.
7. William Haller, *The Rise of Puritanism* (New York: Columbia University Press, 1938), p. 85. For treatment of Puritan worship, see also Horton Davies, *Worship and Theology in England*, 5 vols. (Princeton: Princeton University Press, 1961–75); James Hastings Nichols, *Corporate Worship in the Reformed Tradition* (Philadelphia: The Westminster Press 1968); John H. Leith, *An Introduction to the Reformed Tradition* (Atlanta: John Knox Press, 1977).
8. Robert Bolton, *The Workes of Robert Bolton*, 4 vols. (London, 1639), 2:155; Henry Burton, *A Censure of Simonie* (London, 1624), p. 67; Bolton, 2:136; John Hales, *The Works of John Hales*, 3 vols. (Glasgow, 1765), 3:160; William Prynne, *Histrio-Mastix, The Players Scourge or Actors Tragedy* (London, 1633), Epistle Dedicatory.
9. *St. Austin's Religion* ... (London, 1624), p. 1.
10. Donald McGinn, *The Admonition Controversy* (New Brunswick: Rutgers University Press, 1949), p. 72.
11. Ibid.

12. Richard Stock, *A Stock of Divine Knowledge* (London, 1641), pp. 2ff, 21ff, 175ff, 257.

13. Haller, p. 290.

14. Marthinus Versfeld, *A Guide to the City of God* (London: Sheed and Ward, 1958), p. 59.

15. Richard Sibbes, *The Complete Works of Richard Sibbes*, 6 vols. (London, 1862), 2:194.

16. Bolton, 4:225.

17. Joseph Hall, *The Works of Joseph Hall*, 3 vols. (London, 1628), 3:38.

18. Stock, p. 47.

19. Henry Smith, *The Sermons of Mr. Henry Smith* (London, 1675), p. 93.

20. Hales, 2:45.

21. Sibbes, 3:491.

22. Richard Greenham, *The Workes of the Reverend and Faithful Servant of Jesus Christ M. Richard Greenham* (London, 1612).

23. Ibid., p. 709. See also Richard Bernard, *The Faithful Shepherd* (London, 1621), p. 305.

24. Greenham, p. 746.

25. M. M. Knappen, *Tudor Puritanism* (Chicago: University of Chicago Press, 1939), p. 387.

26. Cf. Sibbes, 2:60ff, 3:137ff, 4:385ff, 5:428ff, 6:114ff; Greenham, pp. 854ff; Hales, 2:217ff, 3:167ff.

27. See, for example, Stock, Bolton, Greenham, and John Robinson, *Observations Divine and Moral* (London, 1851).

28. Greenham, p. 656.

29. Hall, 3:362.

30. Bolton, 2:136.

31. Nicholas Estwick, *A Learned and Godly Sermon at the Funerall of Mr. Robert Bolton* (London, 1635), p. 13.

32. Ibid. John Everard, in instructing his flock on this point, cites Augustine in more detail: "As Augustine speaking of his conversion says, that when he had resolved to forsake his sins, then custom in sin, came and set upon him, says he, all my sins and all my old delights came before me crying unto me, what, will ye leave us now? what, we that have been such old companions, loved so dearly, will you forsake us now? have we not often given you much delight and content and must we now part, and part forever? So part as never to see one another again?" *Some Gospel Treasures Opened* (London, 1653), p. 153.

33. Greenham, p. 753.

34. Ibid., p. 633.

35. Ibid., p. 657.

36. Ibid., p. 800.

37. Burton.

38. Bolton, Vol. 1.

39. See Hall, 1:665; Stock, p. 133; Sibbes, 1:127.

40. Hall, 1:467. See also William Laud, *The Works of Archbishop Laud* (London, 1847), p. 127.

41. Prynne, pp. 49-50. On singing and dancing, he says: "I may joine that of St. Augustine...admonish your neighbors and friends, that they always study to speak that which is honest and good, lest perchance by evil speaking, by dancing upon holy Festivals, and by singing luxurious ribaldry songs, they may seem to inflict wounds upon themselves, even from whence they ought to have praised God. For these unhappy and miserable men, who neither feare or blush to exercise lascivious songs and dances before the very temples of the Saints, although they should come Christians to the Church, because this custome of singing and dancing is but a relique of the observations of the Pagans...consider deare Brethren, whether it be just, that out of that mouth of Christians where the Body of Christ doth enter in, a song should be brought forth, as the very poyson of the devill" (p. 271).

42. Robinson, p. 213. See also Bolton, 2:71.

43. Hall, 1:34. See also Robinson, p. 113; Stock, p. 2.

44. Knappen, p. 367.

Chapter 2

1. Aristotle *Metaphysics* 6.7.338.

2. Ibid., 5.4.222.

3. John Chrysostom *Homiliae Antioch* 4.63; Gregory of Nyssa *Adversus Appolinarem ad Theophilum Episcopum Alexandrinum* 57.1262.

4. Augustine *Contra Epistolam Manichaei quam vocant Fundamenti* 32. Robert West's study has a number of interesting observations on Milton's angels in the light of Augustinian angelology, but he does not enter into a treatment of the creation of the angelic nature nor the possibility of spirit transgression. *Milton and the Angels* (Athens: University of Georgia Press, 1955).

5. Augustine *De Natura Boni contra Manichaeos* 18.

6. Augustine *Contra Epistolam Manichaei quam vocant Fundamenti* 33.36.

7. Augustine *De Moribus Manichaeorum* 4.6.

8. Augustine *Enchiridion ad Laurentium* 10.

9. Augustine *Contra Julianum Opus Imperfectum* 1.206.

10. Augustine *De Civitate Dei* 12.3.

11. Ibid., 22.1.

12. Milton *Christian Doctrine* 7.308.

13. Ibid., 2.131.

14. Ibid., 7.309.

15. Augustine *De Moribus Manichaeorum* 2.3.

16. Milton *Christian Doctrine* 7.310.

17. Ibid., 309.

18. See Camillus Mazella, *De Deo Creante* (Paris, 1877), p. 190.

19. Dom Anscar Vonier, *The Angels* (London: Burns, Oates & Co., 1928), p. 70.

20. Augustine *De Civitate Dei* 11.15.

21. Ibid., 13.

22. Ibid., 15.

23. Ibid., 4.20; 12.1.

24. Jean Danielou in his study of the angels maintains that the "western tradition, after Augustine, holds that the mystery of the Incarnation was known to the angels from the beginning whereas in the East it was manifested that the 'mystery' was hidden to every creature." *The Angels and Their Mission* (Westminster, Md.: Newman Press, 1957), p. 42.

25. Augustine *De Civitate Dei* 14.13.

26. Augustine *De Musica* 6.13.40.

27. Augustine *De Civitate Dei* 14.11.

28. Ibid., 12.1.

29. Ibid., 11.15.

30. Ibid., 12.1.

31. Ibid.

32. Milton *Christian Doctrine* 8.331.

33. Ibid.

34. Ibid., 335.

35. See Roland Mushat Frye, *God, Man, and Satan* (Princeton: Princeton University Press, 1960), pp. 42-85. I am indebted here to Professor Frye for many of his insights on the Augustinian notion of the fall of Satan and the fall of man.

36. Lee A. Jacobus, viewing this in the light of Satan and self-knowledge, points out that Satan "tells us directly that he knows God and that he knows himself," and that Satan "tells us one thing but shows us that he in truth understands quite the opposite." I agree, and the conflict here is the source of his spiritual frustration and mental torment. *Sudden Apprehension: Aspects of Knowledge in Paradise Lost* (The Hague: Mouton & Co., 1976), p. 28.

Chapter 3

1. Augustine *De Civitate Dei* 13.19. For studies of the hexameral tradition, see Watson Kirkconnell's *The Celestial Cycle* (New York: The Gordian Press, 1967); Sr. Mary Irma Corcoran's *Milton's Paradise with Reference to the Hexameral Background* (Washington, D.C.: The Catholic University Press, 1945); and Roland Mushat Frye's recent *Milton's Imagery and the Visual Arts* (Princeton: Princeton University Press, 1978), especially the fine Chapter 15.

Notes

2. Milton *Christian Doctrine* 13.401. See Norman T. Burns, *The Tradition of Christian Mortalism in England: 1530-1660* (Ann Arbor: University of Michigan Press, 1967).

3. Augustine *De Civitate Dei* 14.26.

4. Ibid., 13.23.

5. Augustine *Contra Julianum Opus Imperfectum* 5.1.

6. Irene Samuel, " 'Paradise Lost' as Mimesis," in *Approaches to Paradise Lost*, ed. C. A. Patrides (Toronto: University of Toronto Press, 1968), p. 22. Barbara Lewalski convincingly argues that Edenic life in *Paradise Lost* was radical growth and process, a life steadily increasing in complexity, challenge, and difficulty, but, at the same time, in perfection. "Innocence and Experience in Milton's Eden," in *New Essays on Paradise Lost*, ed. Thomas Kranidas (Berkeley: University of California Press, 1969), p. 88.

7. Denis Saurat, *Milton, Man and Thinker* (London: J. M. Dent & Sons, 1946), p. 227.

8. Augustine *De Civitate Dei* 14.15-27.

9. Ibid., 14.5.

10. Ibid., 12.20.

11. Ibid., 12.10.

12. Ibid., 14.11.

13. See Thomas Aquinas *Summa Theologica* 1.q98, a2, ad3.

14. Augustine *De Civitate Dei* 14.15-26, 16.16, 14.16.

15. Ibid., 14.22.

16. Ibid., 14.23, 15, 16.16, 14.16. "For although conjugal chastity can make a good use of the carnal concupiscence which is in the genital members, yet it has involuntary movements which prove either that it could not exist at all in paradise before sin, or if it did exist, that it was not then such as that it should sometimes resist the will" (*De Trinitate* IX).

17. Augustine *De Doctrina Christiana* 10.

18. Augustine *De Civitate Dei* 14.23.

19. Aquinas *Summa Theologica* 1.q98, a2, ad3.

20. John Carey, *Milton* (London: Evans Brothers Ltd., 1969), p. 107.

21. Dennis Burden, in his excellent treatment of this scene, concludes that Milton "has imposed a regimen that is lacking in Genesis" and his "presentation of life on Earth is developed equally systematically, and its beauty is logical as well as poetic." *The Logical Epic* (London: Routledge & Kegan Paul, 1967), pp. 41-56.

22. Ibid.

23. The Capuchin who supposedly told Addison that Adam could not laugh in the paradisal state because laughter is an effect of Original Sin had a misconception of the gift of impassibility, which allowed Adam and Eve mirth, pleasure, and indeed laughter. Augustine says, "true gladness ceaselessly flowed from the presence of God." *De Civitate Dei* 14.26.

24. Augustine *De Correptione et Gratia* 29.

Notes

25. Augustine *Enarationes in Psalmos* 18.2.2.

26. Milton *Christian Doctrine* 12.394.

27. Grant McColley, *Paradise Lost: An Account of Its Growth and Major Origins* (New York: Russell & Russell, 1963), p. 160.

28. William B. Hunter, "Eve's Demonic Dream," *ELH* 13 (1946):255-65.

29. E. M. W. Tillyard, *Studies in Milton* (London: Chatto & Windus, 1955), pp. 10–12.

30. Ibid.

31. See Kester Svendsen's *Milton and Science* (Cambridge, Mass.: Harvard University Press, 1956), pp. 36–38, for a treatment of the psychology involved in the dream.

32. Augustine *Sermones* 344.a131. For a fine treatment of the psychology of sin in the light of Augustine's explanation of St. Paul, see A. B. Chambers, "The Falls of Adam and Eve in Paradise Lost," in *New Essays on Paradise Lost*, ed. Thomas Kranidas (Berkeley: University of California Press, 1969), pp. 118–30.

33. John S. Diekhoff, "Eve's Dream and the Paradox of Fallible Perfection," *Milton Quarterly* 4 (1970):5-7.

34. Millicent Bell, "The Fallacy of the Fall in *Paradise Lost*," *PMLA* 68 (1953):871.

35. Arnold Stein, *Answerable Style* (Minneapolis: University of Minnesota Press, 1953), p. 93. For a thorough treatment of this scene, see Lee A. Jacobus, *Sudden Apprehension*, p. 33ff. Jacobus agrees that here there is no fall or even a pre-fall: "There is no sin involved here, no genuine fault. What the passage demonstrates is that a greater trust of 'outsides' can lead to deception—at first perhaps innocent but eventually of a serious and grave consequence."

36. Wayne Shumaker, "Notes, Documents and Critical Comments," *PMLA* 70 (1955):1186.

37. Milton *Tetrachordon*, vol. 2, p. 657.

38. Bell, p. 863.

39. Arthur Sewell, *A Study of Milton's Christian Doctrine* (London: Oxford University Press, 1939), p. 146.

40. Bell, p. 863.

41. Edwin Greenlaw, "A Better Teacher than Aquinas," *Studies in Philology* 14 (1917):213.

42. Saurat, p. 128.

43. Ibid., p. 129.

44. Augustine *De Civitate Dei* 14.11. The late Professor A. S. P. Woodhouse, in referring to this teaching in the *City of God*, maintains that Augustine here offers no solution to the problem of motivation in the Fall, whereas the epic does. *The Heavenly Muse*, ed. Hugh MacCallum (Toronto: University of Toronto Press, 1972), p. 259. I contend that Milton's solution is due largely to his understanding of this teaching as it appears not only in *City of God*, but also in the Father's more detailed treatment in *De Correptione et Gratia* and his other commen-

taries on Genesis. "The free disposition of the will was the cause of our doing ill, as the just judgment was the cause of our suffering ill" (*Confessiones* 10).

45. Augustine *De Correptione et Gratia* 10.26.

Chapter 4

1. Professor Rama Sarma's observation that Milton "does not very much harp on Original Sin, only once he uses the expression to show the authenticity of the biblical version of the Fall in the epic" is naive. The teaching and all its ramifications, regardless of how often the expression is used, is at the heart of the epic's theology. *The Heroic Argument: A Study of Milton's Heroic Poetry* (Madras: Macmillan & Co. Ltd., 1971), p. 52.

2. Augustine *De Civitate Dei* 14.12.

3. Augustine *Enchiridion ad Laurentium* 45.

4. Milton *Christian Doctrine* 11.383-84.

5. E. L. Marilla, "The Central Problem of *Paradise Lost*: The Fall of Man," reprinted in *Milton and Modern Man* (University: University of Alabama Press, 1967), p. 31.

6. Augustine *De Genesi ad Litteram* 6.15; *Epistolae* 4.3; *De Natura et Gratia* 25; *Enchiridion* 25.

7. Milton *Christian Doctrine* 12.393.

8. Ibid., 393.

9. Ibid., 13.399.

10. Ibid., 12.394.

11. Augustine *De Gratia et Libero Arbitrio* 10.

12. Augustine *De Correptione et Gratia* 32.

13. Milton *Christian Doctrine* 12.394.

14. Ibid., 395.

15. Ibid.

16. Ibid.

17. Augustine *De Civitate Dei* 14.17. See also, *Tractatus in Joannis Evangelium* 3.12; *De Nuptiis et Concupiscentia* 1.7; Gen. iii.7: "They knew that they were naked" and "they sewed leaves together and made themselves aprons."

18. Milton *Christian Doctrine* 11.383.

19. Ibid., 388.

20. Ibid.

21. Ibid.

22. Ibid., 383.

23. Augustine *De Correptione et Gratia* 29.

24. Ibid.

25. Augustine *Enarationes in Psalmos* 18.2.2.

26. Augustine *De Genesi ad Litteram* 6.15.

27. Augustine *De Civitate Dei* 18.2.

Notes

28. William J. Grace, *Ideas in Milton* (Notre Dame: University of Notre Dame Press, 1968), p. 3.
29. Ibid.
30. Augustine *Contra Duas Epistolas Pelagianorum* 2.8; *Contra Julianum Opus Imperfectum* 3.190; *Contra Julianum Libri Sex* 4.14; *De Civitate Dei* 12.3.
31. J. M. Evans, *Paradise Lost and the Genesis Tradition* (Oxford: The Clarendon Press, 1968).
32. Milton *Christian Doctrine* 12.396.
33. Ibid.
34. Ibid.
35. Ibid., 397.
36. Ibid., 4.186.
37. Augustine calls this converting grace. See *De Gratia et Libero Arbitrio* 24.
38. See also John Chrysostom *In 1 Corinthianos* 8; Athanasius *In Contra Arianos* 70; Tertullian *De Poenitentia*.
39. Augustine *De Civitate Dei* 13.14. Also *Enchiridion* 26.
40. Augustine *De Civitate Dei* 12.21. Helpful in clarifying the mystery of corporateness is the word Adam in its original Hebrew sense, which carried with it not only the meaning that man had come from earth, but also that the first creature was undifferentiated in regard to sex.
41. Ibid., 13.3.
42. Ibid., 13.14.
43. Milton *Christian Doctrine* 11.391.
44. Ibid., 384.
45. Ibid.
46. Ibid., 385.
47. Since F. T. Prince's early defense of Books XI and XII ("On the Last Two Books of Paradise Lost," *Essays and Studies*, n.s. 11 [1958]), some excellent studies on the relative merits of the books have appeared. See, particularly, Mary Ann Radinowicz's " 'Man as a Probationer of Immortality': Paradise Lost XI-XII," in *Approaches to Paradise Lost*, ed. C. A. Patrides (Toronto: University of Toronto Press, 1968), pp. 31-51; and M. Christopher Pecheux, O. S. U., "The Second Adam and the Church in Paradise Lost," in *Critical Essays on Milton in ELH* (Baltimore: The Johns Hopkins Press, 1969), pp. 195-209.

Chapter 5

1. For a thorough investigation of Milton's doctrine of the Incarnation, see William B. Hunter, Jr., "Milton on the Incarnation," in *Bright Essence* (Salt Lake City: University of Utah Press, 1971), pp. 131-48.
2. Augustine *De Catechizandis Rudibus* 26.52.

3. Milton *Christian Doctrine* 14.418, 424.
4. Augustine *Epistolae* 2.8.
5. Milton *Christian Doctrine* 14.426.
6. Augustine *Epistolae* 2.4.
7. Milton *Christian Doctrine* 14.427-28.
8. Augustine *Epistolae* 11.4.
9. Milton *Christian Doctrine* 14.424.
10. Augustine *Enchiridion* 10.34.
11. Ibid., 11.36.
12. Milton *Christian Doctrine* 14.423.
13. Augustine *Enarationes in Psalmos* 88.2. Also *Psalmos* 136.8.
14. Milton *Christian Doctrine* 14.417.
15. Augustine *De Trinitate* 4.14 (19).
16. Milton *Christian Doctrine* 14.426.
17. Augustine *Sermones* 336, 263, 172.2, 304.2.
18. Milton *Christian Doctrine* 14.415.
19. See Peter A. Fiore, " 'Account Mee Man': The Incarnation in Paradise Lost," *The Huntington Library Quarterly* 39 (1975):51.
20. Ibid.
21. Augustine *De Nuptiis et Concupiscentia* 1.21.
22. Ibid.
23. Milton *Christian Doctrine* 29.566.
24. Ibid., 24.500.
25. Ibid. See also Milton's *Reason and Church Government*, vol. 2, p. 755; *Tetrachordon*, vol. 2, p. 606; *Colasterion*, vol. 2, p. 739. The response to Hugh MacCallum's query, "One wonders what effect Raphael's revelation of the distinction of Father and Son would have had on Adam if he had remained in his unfallen state," is that Adam would have accepted the Son as glorified king on earth, since there would be no redemptive role for the Son to exercise. " 'Most Perfect Hero': The Role of the Son in Milton's Theodicy," in *Paradise Lost: A Tercentenary Tribute*, ed. Balachandra Rajan (Toronto: University of Toronto Press, 1969), p. 87.
26. Milton *Christian Doctrine* 14.419.
27. Augustine *De Peccato Originali* 1.26.
28. Augustine *Enchiridion* 108. I Tim. ii.6: "Who gave himself a ransom for all."
29. Milton *Christian Doctrine* 14.428.
30. Ibid., 426.
31. Ibid., 2.134.
32. Ibid., 3.154.
33. Augustine *Enchiridion* 35; *De Peccato Originali* 33.
34. Augustine *Sermones* 47.21.
35. Milton *Christian Doctrine* 14.418.
36. Ibid., 5.225-26.
37. Augustine *De Peccato Originali* 28.33.
38. Augustine *De Trinitate* 4.14.
39. Milton *Christian Doctrine* 15.430.

Notes

40. Augustine *Enarationes in Psalmos* 2.7; *Tractatus in Joannis Evangelium* 41; *Quaestionum Evangeliorum Libri Duo* 1.34; *Contra Adversarium Legis et Prophetarum* 1.18(37). Luke x.22: "No man knoweth who the Son is but the Father; and who the Father is, but the Son, and he to whom the Son will reveal him"; and Heb. v.10: "Called by God an high priest after the order of Melchisedec"; and Rev. xix.16: "King of Kings, and Lord of Lords."

41. Milton *Christian Doctrine* 15.432.

42. Ibid.

43. Ibid., 433. Psal. cx.4: "Thou art a priest forever after the order of Melchizedek."

44. Ibid., 14.426.

45. Ibid., 428.

46. Ibid., 419.

47. Ibid., 5.206.

48. Ibid., 20.475.

49. Ibid., 15.437.

50. Ibid., 2.143. It should be mentioned here that there is a certain confusion in Milton's teaching on the concept of eternity and his understanding of John's text "In the beginning...." The expression "In the beginning..." does suggest, no matter how you look at it, that in a particular period of time something began. The idea of eternity, on the other hand, suggests no time at all, or a period well before anything that has a beginning: eternity is that which has no beginning and no end (p. 143). Milton doesn't really resolve this particular contradiction; he simply equates "In the beginning..." with eternity while he says we shouldn't. Despite the fact that he insists that "In the beginning..." does not in any way mean eternity (pp. 238-39), and that John's verse "he was in the beginning with" in no way proves that Christ is of the same essence with God but simply proves that Christ "was with, or in company with God" (p. 239), he proceeds to teach that the prophetic function was from the beginning (15.434) and the priestly function was from the beginning (15.475); then, in the very same context, he says that the kingly and priestly functions are eternal (15.437).

51. Ibid., 15.435.

52. Ibid., 437.

53. Ibid., 33.627.

54. Howard Schultz, "Christ and Antichrist in Paradise Regained," *PMLA* 67 (1952):806-7.

55. Barbara Lewalski, *Milton's Brief Epic* (Providence: Brown University Press, 1966), p. 314.

56. Milton *Christian Doctrine* 16.438. Phil. ii.6-8: "Took upon himself the form of a servant...he humbled himself, and became obedient unto death."

57. Ibid., 16.440.

58. Ibid., 15.434.

59. Augustine *De Trinitate* IV.

60. Milton *Christian Doctrine* 16.439-40.

61. Ibid., 16.443. Rom. viii.3-4: "That the righteousness of the law might be fulfilled in us."
62. Ibid., 444.
63. Ibid., 22.486.
64. Augustine *De Libero Arbitrio* 3.10, 31.
65. See Chapter 2 of this study.
66. Augustine *De Trinitate* 4 and 13. Also *Enchiridion*.
67. Augustine *De Trinitate* 4.19.
68. Anselm *Cur Deus Homo* 1.9-10.
69. Milton *Christian Doctrine* 16.446.
70. Ibid., 447-48.
71. Ibid., 22.490.
72. Augustine *Sermones* 4.
73. Milton *Christian Doctrine* 15.435.
74. Augustine *Epistolae* 155.
75. Ibid.
76. Augustine *Enarationes in Psalmos* 125.1.
77. Milton *Christian Doctrine* 15.436.
78. B. Rajan, *Paradise Lost and the Seventeenth Century Reader* (New York: Oxford University Press, 1948), pp. 47-50; Ernest Schanzer, "Milton's Hell Revisited," *University of Toronto Quarterly* 24 (1955): 136-46; Irene Samuel, "The Dialogue in Heaven: A Reconsideration of Paradise Lost, 3, 1-417," *PMLA* 72 (1947):601-11; J. B. Broadbent, *Some Graver Subject* (London: Chatto & Windus, 1960), p. 111.
79. Merritt Y. Hughes, *Ten Perspectives on Milton* (New Haven: Yale University Press, 1965), p. 106.
80. John Peter, *A Critique of Paradise Lost* (New York: Columbia University Press, 1960), p. 12. For an excellent appraisal of the dramatic role which the Father adopts in Book III and the role the Son accepts as freely loving and responding to the Father's merciful purposes, see Stella P. Revard, "The Dramatic Function of the Son in Paradise Lost: A Commentary on Milton's 'Trinitarianism'," *Journal of English and Germanic Philology* 66 (1967):45-58; and Arthur E. Barker, "Paradise Lost: The Relevance of Regeneration," in *Paradise Lost: A Tercentenary Tribute*, ed. Balachandra Rajan (Toronto: University of Toronto Press, 1969), pp. 48-78.
81. In support of Stanley Fish's reading of *Paradise Lost*, I am convinced that the reader's awareness and education of the three offices of Christ actually account for the Son's being the more successful. *Surprised by Sin* (Berkeley: University of California Press, 1971). C. A. Patrides says that the God-man in *Paradise Lost* renders coherence to the whole epic. *Milton and the Christian Tradition* (Oxford: The Clarendon Press, 1966), p. 260.
82. The misunderstanding that Milton was an Arian has been admirably corrected by William B. Hunter, Jr., in "Milton's Arianism Reconsidered," pp. 29-51. Hunter's conclusion that Milton subscribes to a subordinationist theory in Trinitarian matters, which is vastly different from Arianism, is supported by J. D. Adamson in "Milton's

Notes

Arianism," pp. 53-61, and C. A. Patrides in "Milton and Arianism," pp. 63-70; all three articles are in *Bright Essence*.

83. C. A. Patrides, "The Godhead in Paradise Lost: Dogma or Drama," in *Bright Essence*, p. 74.

84. Harry Blamires, *Milton's Creation* (London: Methuen & Co. Ltd, 1971), p. 68.

85. Augustine *Enarationes in Psalmos* 88.2.

86. Milton *Christian Doctrine* 14.415-16.

87. Augustine *Enarationes in Psalmos* 58; *Sermones* 1.7.

88. Augustine *De Agone Christiano* 11.12.

89. Milton *Christian Doctrine* 16.438.

90. Augustine *Sermones* 22.10, 246.4; and *De Doctrina Christiana* 1.34, 38.

91. Milton *Christian Doctrine* 16.440.

92. Augustine *De Trinitate* 13.16.

93. Milton *Christian Doctrine* 14.426, and 16.449.

94. Augustine *Enchiridion* 51.

95. Milton *Christian Doctrine* 16.445.

96. Augustine *Enchiridion* 51.

97. Milton *Christian Doctrine* 16.447.

98. Ibid., 17.454.

99. Augustine *Enchiridion* 51.

100. Milton *Christian Doctrine* 21.477.

101. Augustine *Enchiridion* 50.

102. Milton *Christian Doctrine* 14.415.

103. Arthur O. Lovejoy's recommendation that the two themes be kept separate in understanding the paradox is still the most sensible solution. He says: "In the part of the narrative dealing primarily with the Fall, the thought that it was after all a felix culpa must not be permitted explicitly to intrude; that was to be reserved for the conclusion, where it could heighten the happy final consummation by making the earlier and unhappy episodes in the story appear as instrumental necessary conditions." "Milton and the Paradox of the Fortunate Fall," in *Critical Essays on Milton in ELH* (Baltimore: Johns Hopkins Press, 1969), p. 181, originally printed in September 1937, vol. 4. Frank L. Huntley sees the *felix culpa* in the light of the larger pattern of systasis that Milton employs in *Paradise Lost*; "Before and After the Fall: Some Miltonic Patterns of Systasis," in *Approaches to Paradise Lost*, ed. C. A. Patrides (Toronto: University of Toronto Press, 1968). Lawrence W. Hyman sees the fortunate fall as part of the rhythmic pattern of light and darkness, upward and downward movements, "the mythic rather than the logical aspects of Christianity" in the poem; *The Quarrel Within* (Port Washington: Kennikat Press, 1972), p. 57. See also Earl Miner's very sensitive appraisal of the question in "Felix Culpa in the Redemptive Order of Paradise Lost," *Philological Quarterly* 47 (1968): 43-54.

Bibliography

Bibliographical Note

All passages from *Paradise Lost* are from the Odyssey Press edition (New York, 1957), edited by Merritt Y. Hughes. All citations from Milton's *Christian Doctrine* are from *The Complete Prose Works of John Milton*, Volume 6, edited by Maurice Kelley, translated by John Carey (New Haven: Yale University Press, 1973). Other citations from Milton's prose are also from the Yale edition (6 volumes, 1953-1973). The occasional Latin quotations from *De Doctrina Christiana* are from *The Works of John Milton*, Volumes 14-17, general editor Frank A. Patterson (New York: Columbia University Press, 1931-40).

For the works of Augustine, I have used J.-P. Migne, *Patrologiae, Cursus Completus*, series latina (New York: Adler's Foreign Books, 1965-71); citations from other Church Fathers are from Migne as well. Quotations of Augustine in English are pretty much my own translation, although I have used *The City of God*, edited by R. V. Tasker, translated by John Healey (New York: E. P. Dutton/Everyman's Library edition) for verification.

Biblical quotations are from the Authorized Version and the English Revised Version.

Augustine Works

Confessiones
Contra Adversarium Legis et Prophetarum
Contra Duas Epistolas Pelagianorum
Contra Epistolam Manichaei quam vocant Fundamenti
Contra Faustum Manichaeum Libri Triginta Tres
Contra Julianum Libri Sex
Contra Julianum Opus Imperfectum
De Agone Christiano
De Catechizandis Rudibus
De Civitate Dei
De Correptione et Gratia
De Doctrina Christiana
De Duabus Animabus contra Minichaeos
De Genesi ad Litteram
De Genesi contra Manichaeos
De Gratia et Libero Arbitrio

Bibliography

De Libero Arbitrio
De Moribus Manichaeorum
De Musica Libri Sex
De Natura Boni contra Manichaeos
De Natura et Gratia contra Pelagium
De Nuptiis et Concupiscentia
De Ordine
De Peccato Originali
De Trinitate
Enarationes in Psalmos
Enchiridion ad Laurentium
Epistolae
Liber de Diversis Quaestionibus 83
Liber de Diversis Quaestionibus ad Simplicianum Libri Duo
Quaestionum Evangeliorum Libri Duo
Sermones
Tractatus in Joannis Evangelium

Works Cited and Consulted

Abercrombie, Nigel. *Saint Augustine and French Classical Thought.* Oxford: The Clarendon Press, 1938.

Adamson, J. D. "Milton's Arianism." In *Bright Essence*, pp. 53–61. Salt Lake City: University of Utah Press, 1971.

Allen, Don Cameron. *The Harmonious Vision.* Baltimore: Johns Hopkins Press, 1970.

———. "Milton and the Descent of Light." *Journal of English and Germanic Philology* 60 (1961):614–30.

Ames, William. *The Marrow of Sacred Divinity.* London, 1642.

Anselm. *Cur Deus Homo.* Chicago: The Open Court Publishing Co., 1948.

Athanasius. *In Contra Arianos.* Patrologiae Cursus Completus, J.-P. Migne, series graeca.

Barker, Arthur E. "Milton's Schoolmasters." *Modern Language Review* 32 (1937):517–36.

———. "Paradise Lost: The Relevance of Regeneration." In *Paradise Lost: A Tercentenary Tribute*, edited by B. Rajan, pp. 48–78. Toronto: University of Toronto Press, 1969.

Bell, Millicent. "The Fallacy of the Fall in *Paradise Lost*." *PMLA* 68 (1953):863–83.

Bernard, Richard. *The Faithful Shepherd.* London, 1621.

Blamires, Harry. *Milton's Creation.* London: Methuen & Co., Ltd., 1971.

Bolton, Robert. *The Workes of Robert Bolton.* 4 vols. London, 1639.

Broadbent, J. B. *Some Graver Subject.* London: Chatto & Windus, 1960.

Burden, Dennis H. *The Logical Epic.* London: Routledge & Kegan Paul, 1967.

Bibliography

Burns, Norman T. *The Tradition of Christian Mortalism in England: 1530-1660.* Ann Arbor: University of Michigan Press, 1967.

Burton, Henry. *A Censure of Simonie.* London, 1624.

Bush, Douglas. *"Paradise Lost" in Our Time: Some Comments.* Gloucester, Mass.: Peter Smith, 1957.

Calvin, John. *Institutio Christianae Religionis.* Philadelphia: Westminster Press, 1960.

Carey, John. *Milton.* London: Evans Brothers, Ltd., 1969.

Chambers, A. B. "The Falls of Adam and Eve in *Paradise Lost*." In *New Essays on Paradise Lost*, edited by Thomas Kranidas, pp. 118-30. Berkeley: University of California Press, 1969.

Clark, Donald L. *John Milton at St. Paul's School.* New York: Columbia University Press, 1948.

Colie, Rosalie. "Time and Eternity: Paradox and Structure in *Paradise Lost*." *Journal of the Warburg and Courtauld Institute* 23 (1960): 127-38.

Corcoran, Sr. Mary Irma. *Milton's Paradise with Reference to the Hexameral Background.* Washington, D.C.: Catholic University Press, 1945.

Daiches, David. *Milton.* London: Hutchinson University Press, 1957.

Danielou, Jean. *The Angels and Their Mission.* Westminster, Md.: Newman Press, 1957.

Davies, Horton. *Worship and Theology in England.* 5 vols. Princeton: Princeton University Press, 1961-75.

Diekhoff, John S. "Eve's Dream and the Paradox of Fallible Perfection." *Milton Quarterly* 4 (1970):5-7.

Duncan, Joseph E. *Milton's Earthly Paradise: A Historical Study.* Minneapolis: University of Minnesota Press, 1972.

Duns Scotus, Joannes. *Philosophical Writings.* Edited and translated by Allan Wolter. Indianapolis: Bobbs Merrill, 1964.

Empson, William. *Milton's God.* London: Chatto & Windus, 1961.

Estwick, Nicholas. *A Learned and Godly Sermon at the Funerall of Mr. Robert Bolton.* London, 1635.

Evans, J. M. *Paradise Lost and the Genesis Tradition.* Oxford: The Clarendon Press, 1968.

Everard, John. *Some Gospel Treasures Opened.* London, 1653.

Ferry, Anne Davidson. *Milton's Epic Voice: The Narrator in Paradise Lost.* Cambridge, Mass.: Harvard University Press, 1963.

Fiore, Peter A. " 'Account Mee Man': The Incarnation in *Paradise Lost*." *The Huntington Library Quarterly* 39 (1975):51-56.

Fish, Stanley. *Surprised by Sin.* Berkeley: University of California Press, 1971.

Frye, Northrop. *The Return of Eden.* Toronto: University of Toronto Press, 1965.

Frye, Roland Mushat. *God, Man, and Satan.* Princeton: Princeton University Press, 1960.

―――― . *Milton's Imagery and the Visual Arts.* Princeton: Princeton University Press, 1978.

Bibliography

Gardner, Helen. *A Reading of Paradise Lost.* Oxford: The Clarendon Press, 1965.

Gilbert, Allan H. *On the Composition of Paradise Lost.* Chapel Hill: University of North Carolina Press, 1947.

Grace, William J. *Ideas in Milton.* Notre Dame: University of Notre Dame Press, 1968.

Greenham, Richard. *The Workes of the Reverend and Faithful Servant of Jesus Christ M. Richard Greenham.* London, 1612.

Greenlaw, Edwin. "A Better Teacher than Aquinas." *Studies in Philology* 14 (1917):196-217.

Gregory of Nyssa. *Adversus Appolinarem ad Theophilum Episcopum Alexandrinum.* Patrologiae Cursus Completus, J.-P Migne, series graeca.

Grierson, Herbert J. C. *Milton and Wordsworth.* London: Chatto & Windus, 1950.

Hales, John. *The Works of John Hales.* 3 vols. Glasgow, 1765.

Hall, Joseph. *The Works of Joseph Hall.* 3 vols. London, 1628.

Haller, William. *The Rise of Puritanism.* New York: Columbia University Press, 1938.

Hughes, Merritt Y. *Ten Perspectives on Milton.* New Haven: Yale University Press, 1965.

Hunter, William B., Jr. "Eve's Demonic Dream." *ELH* 13 (1946): 255-65.

──────. "Milton's Arianism Reconsidered." In *Bright Essence,* pp. 29-51. Salt Lake City: University of Utah Press, 1971.

──────. "Milton on the Incarnation." In *Bright Essence,* pp. 131-48. Salt Lake City: University of Utah Press, 1971.

Huntley, Frank L. "Before and After the Fall: Some Miltonic Patterns of Systasis." In *Approaches to Paradise Lost,* edited by C. A. Patrides, pp. 1-14. Toronto: University of Toronto Press, 1968.

Hyman, Lawrence W. *The Quarrel Within.* Port Washington: Kennikat Press, 1972.

Jacobus, Lee A. *Sudden Apprehension: Aspects of Knowledge in Paradise Lost.* The Hague: Mouton & Co., 1976.

John Chrysostom. *Homiliae Antioch.* Patrologiae Cursus Completus, J.-P. Migne, series graeca.

──────. *In 1 Corinthianos.* J.-P. Migne.

Kelley, Maurice. *This Great Argument.* Gloucester, Mass.: Peter Smith, 1962.

──────. "Milton's Arianism Reconsidered." *Harvard Theological Review* 54 (1961):195-205.

Kermode, Frank. "Adam Unparadised." In *The Living Milton,* edited by Frank Kermode, pp. 85-123. London: Routledge & Kegan Paul, 1960.

Kerrigan, William. "The Heretical Milton: From Assumption to Mortalism." *English Literary Renaissance* 5 (1975):125-66.

Kirkconnell, Watson. *The Celestial Cycle: The Theme of Paradise Lost in World Literature, with Translations of the Major Analogues.* New York: The Gordian Press, 1967.

Bibliography

Kivette, Ruth M. "Milton on the Trinity." Ph.D. dissertation, Columbia University, 1960.

Knappen, M. M. *Tudor Puritanism*. Chicago: University of Chicago Press, 1939.

Kurth, Burton O. *Milton and Christian Heroism*. Hamden, Conn.: Anchor Books, 1966.

Labriola, Albert C. "The Aesthetics of Self-Diminution: Christian Iconography in *Paradise Lost*." *Milton Studies* 7 (1975):267-311.

Landy, Marcia. "Kinship and the Role of Women in *Paradise Lost*." *Milton Studies* 4 (1972):3-18.

Laud, William. *The Works of Archbishop Laud*. London, 1847.

Leach, A. F. "Milton as Schoolboy and Schoolmaster." *Proceedings of the British Academy* 3 (1908):295-318.

LeComte, Edward S. *Yet Once More*. New York: Columbia University Press, 1953.

──────. *Milton and Sex*. New York: Columbia University Press, 1978.

Leith, John H. *An Introduction to the Reformed Tradition*. Atlanta: John Knox Press, 1977.

Lewalski, Barbara K. "Innocence and Experience in Milton's Eden." In *New Essays on Paradise Lost*, edited by Thomas Kranidas, pp. 86-117. Berkeley: University of California Press, 1969.

──────. *Milton's Brief Epic*. Providence: Brown University Press, 1966.

Lewis, C. S. *A Preface to Paradise Lost*. London: Oxford University Press, 1942.

Lieb, Michael. *The Dialectics of Creation: Patterns of Birth and Regeneration in Paradise Lost*. Amherst: University of Massachusetts Press, 1970.

Lovejoy, Arthur O. "Milton and the Paradox of the Fortunate Fall." In *Critical Essays on Milton in ELH*, pp. 163-81. Baltimore: Johns Hopkins Press, 1969.

Low, Anthony. "Milton's God: Authority in *Paradise Lost*." *Milton Studies* 4 (1972):19-38.

Lupton, Joseph H. *Life of Dean Colet*. London: George Bell & Sons, 1909.

MacCaffrey, Isabel. *"Paradise Lost" as Myth*. Cambridge, Mass.: Harvard University Press, 1959.

MacCallum, Hugh. " 'Most Perfect Hero': The Role of the Son in Milton's Theodicy." In *Paradise Lost: A Tercentenary Tribute*, edited by B. Rajan, pp. 79-105. Toronto: University of Toronto Press, 1969.

Madsen, William. *From Shadowy Types to Truth*. New Haven: Yale University Press, 1968.

Marilla, E. L. "The Central Problem of *Paradise Lost*: The Fall of Man." Reprinted in *Milton and Modern Man*, pp. 27-55. University: University of Alabama Press, 1968.

Martz, Louis. *The Paradise Within*. New Haven: Yale University Press, 1964.

Mazella, Camillus, *De Deo Creante*. Paris, 1877.

McColley, Grant. *Paradise Lost: An Account of Its Growth and Major Origins*. New York: Russell & Russell, 1963.

Bibliography

McGinn, Donald. *The Admonition Controversy*. New Brunswick: Rutgers University Press, 1949.

Miner, Earl. "Felix Culpa in the Redemptive Order of *Paradise Lost*." *Philological Quarterly* 47 (1968):43–54.

Mollenkott, Virginia. "Milton's Rejection of the Fortunate Fall." *Milton Quarterly* 6 (1972):1–5.

Nichols, James Hastings. *Corporate Worship in the Reformed Tradition*. Philadelphia: The Westminster Press, 1968.

Nicolson, Marjorie Hope. *John Milton: A Reader's Guide to his Poetry*. New York: Farrar, Straus, 1963.

Parish, John. "Milton and an Anthropomorphic God." *Studies in Philology* 56 (1959):619–25.

Parker, William Riley. *Milton: A Biography*. 2 vols. New York: Oxford University Press, 1968.

Patrick, J. Max. "A Reconsideration of the Fall of Eve." *Etudes Anglaises* 28 (1975):15–21.

Patrides, C. A. "The Godhead in *Paradise Lost*: Dogma or Drama." In *Bright Essence*, pp. 71-77. Salt Lake City: University of Utah Press, 1971.

————. "Milton and Arianism." In *Bright Essence*, 1971, pp. 63–70.

————. *Milton and the Christian Tradition*. Oxford: The Clarendon Press, 1966.

Pecheux, M. Christopher, O.S.U. "The Second Adam and the Church in *Paradise Lost*." In *Critical Essays on Milton in ELH*, pp. 195–209. Baltimore: Johns Hopkins Press, 1969.

Peter, John. *A Critique of Paradise Lost*. New York: Columbia University Press, 1960.

Prince, F. T. "On the Last Two Books of *Paradise Lost*." *Essays and Studies* 11 (1958):38–52.

Prynne, William. *Histrio-Mastix, The Players Scourge or Actors Tragedy*. London, 1633.

Radinowicz, Mary Ann. " 'Man as Probationer of Immortality': *Paradise Lost* XI-XII." In *Approaches to Paradise Lost*, edited by C. A. Patrides, pp. 31–51. Toronto: University of Toronto Press, 1968.

Rajan, B. *Paradise Lost and the Seventeenth Century Reader*. New York: Oxford University Press, 1948.

Rama Sarma, M.V. *The Heroic Argument: A Study of Milton's Heroic Poetry*. Madras: Macmillan & Co., Ltd., 1971.

Revard, Stella. "The Dramatic Function of the Son in *Paradise Lost*: A Commentary on Milton's 'Trinitarianism'." *Journal of English and Germanic Philology* 66 (1967):45–58.

————. "Satan's Envy of the Kingship of the Son of God: A Reconsideration of *Paradise Lost*, Book 5, and Its Theological Background." *Modern Philology* 70 (1973):190–98.

Ricks, Christopher. *Milton's Grand Style*. Oxford: The Clarendon Press, 1963.

Bibliography

Riggs, William G. *The Christian Poet in Paradise Lost.* Berkeley: University of California Press, 1972.

Robinson, John. *Observations Divine and Moral.* London, 1851.

St. Austin's Religion wherein is manifestly proved out of the Works of that Learned Father, that he dissented from Popery, and agreed with the Religion of the Protestants in all the main Points of Faith and Doctrine—Contrary to the Impudent, Erroneous, and Slanderous Position of the bragging Papists of our Times, who falsely affirme, we had no Religion before the times of Luther and Calvine. London, 1624.

Samuel, Irene. "The Dialogue in Heaven: A Reconsideration of *Paradise Lost,* 3, 1-147." *PMLA* 72 (1947):601-11.

————. " 'Paradise Lost' as Mimesis." In *Approaches to Paradise Lost,* edited by C. A. Patrides, pp. 15-29. Toronto: University of Toronto Press, 1968.

Saurat, Denis. *Milton, Man and Thinker.* London: J. M. Dent & Sons, 1946.

Schanzer, Ernest. "Milton's Hell Revisited." *University of Toronto Quarterly* 24 (1955):136-45.

Schultz, Howard. "Christ and Antichrist in *Paradise Regained.*" *PMLA* 67 (1952):790-808.

Sewell, Arthur. *A Study of Milton's Christian Doctrine.* London: Oxford University Press, 1939.

Shawcross, John T. "The Metaphor of Inspiration in *Paradise Lost.*" In *Th'Upright Heart and Pure,* edited by P. A. Fiore, pp. 75-85. Pittsburgh: Duquesne University Press, 1967.

————. "The Rhetor as Creator in *Paradise Lost.*" *Milton Studies* 8 (1975):209-19.

Shumaker, Wayne. "Notes, Documents and Critical Comments." *PMLA* 70 (1955):1185-87.

————. *Unpremeditated Verse.* Princeton: Princeton University Press, 1967.

Sibbes, Richard. *The Complete Works of Richard Sibbes.* 6 vols. London, 1862.

Sims, James H. *The Bible in Milton's Epics.* Gainesville: University of Florida Press, 1962.

Smith, Henry. *The Sermons of Mr. Henry Smith.* London, 1675.

Steadman, John M. "Adam and the Prophesied Redeemer." *Studies in Philology* 56 (1959):214-25.

————. "Milton and Patristic Tradition: The Quality of Hell-fire." *Anglia* 76 (1958):116-28.

————. *Milton and the Renaissance Hero.* Oxford: The Clarendon Press, 1967.

Stein, Arnold. *Answerable Style.* Minneapolis: University of Minnesota Press, 1953.

Stock, Richard. *A Stock of Divine Knowledge, being a lively description of the Divine Nature.* London, 1641.

Bibliography

————. *The Churches Lamentation for the Losse of the Godly.* London, 1614.

Summers, Joseph. *The Muse's Method.* Cambridge, Mass.: Harvard University Press, 1962.

Svendsen, Kester. *Milton and Science.* Cambridge, Mass.: Harvard University Press, 1956.

Tertullian. *De Poenitentia.* Patrologiae Cursus Completus, J.-P. Migne, series latina.

Thomas Aquinas. *Summa Theologica.* New York: Benziger Bros., 1947–48.

Tillyard, E. M. W. *Studies in Milton.* London: Chatto & Windus, 1955.

Ulreich, John C., Jr. "A Paradise Within: The Fortunate Fall in *Paradise Lost.*" *Journal of the History of Ideas* 32 (1971):351–66.

Van Doren, Mark. *The Noble Voice.* New York: Henry Holt & Co., 1946.

Versfeld, Marthinus. *A Guide to the City of God.* London: Sheed & Ward, 1958.

Vonier, Dom Anscar. *The Angels.* London: Burns, Oates & Co., 1928.

Waldock, A. J. A. *Paradise Lost and its Critics.* Cambridge: The University Press, 1961.

Watson, Foster. *The English Grammar Schools to 1660: Their curriculum and practice.* Cambridge: The University Press, 1908.

West, Robert. *Milton and the Angels.* Athens: University of Georgia Press, 1955.

Whiting, George. *Milton and this Pendant World.* Austin: University of Texas Press, 1958.

Williams, Arnold. *The Common Expositor.* Chapel Hill: University of North Carolina Press, 1948.

Wittreich, Joseph Anthony, Jr. " 'A Poet Amongst Poets': Milton and the Tradition of Prophecy." In *Milton and the Line of Vision,* edited by Joseph Anthony Wittreich, Jr., pp. 97-142. Madison: University of Wisconsin Press, 1974.

Wolfson, Harry Austryn. *The Philosophy of the Church Fathers.* Cambridge, Mass.: Harvard University Press, 1976.

Woodhouse, A. S. P. *The Heavenly Muse.* Edited by Hugh MacCallum. Toronto: University of Toronto Press, 1972.

Wright, B. A. *Milton's "Paradise Lost."* New York: Barnes & Noble, 1962.

Index

Abel, 46
Abercrombie, Nigel, 95
Abstinence, 43
Accidents, 12, 13, 54
Adamson, J.D., 105
Addison, 60, 99
Adequate, 62, 89, 92
Admonition Controversy, The, 4, 95
Adoption, 47
Adoration, 75, 77
Agag, 59
Allhallows, 5
Ambition, 50
Ambrose, 7
Ames, William, 4
Angelology, 13, 15-22, 97
Anger, 51, 68, 74
Anselm, 70, 80, 81
Aquinas, Thomas, 30, 99, 100
Areopagitica, 36
Arianism, 105, 106
Aristotle, 13, 97
Athanasius, 102
Atonement, 63, 80, 86
Avarice, 44

Babylon, 19
Barker, Arthur E., 2, 105
Beatific Vision, 27
Beatitude, 16
Beelzebub, 17
Bell, Millicent, 37, 38
Bernard, Richard, 96
Blamires, Harry, 87
Bolton, Robert, 6, 9, 10, 95, 96, 97
Bonaventure, 66
Broadbent, J. B., 85
Burden, Dennis H., 32, 99
Burns, Norman T., 99
Burton, Henry, 10, 95

Cain, 46
Calvin, John, 3, 79
Cambridge Platonists, The, 12
Canonization, The, 31
Carey, John, 31
Cartwright, Thomas, 4
Chambers, A. B., 100
Charity, 57, 84
Christology, 61, 72
Chrysostom, John, 97, 102
Church, The, 7, 10, 61, 63, 65, 66, 72, 76, 82, 83, 84, 85, 97, 102
Colasterion, 103
Colet, John, 2
Command, 38, 42, 43
Commonplace Book, The, 2
Comus, 36
Concupiscence, 26, 28, 30, 31, 39, 48-53, 79, 99
Confesio Augustiniana, 3
Conscience, 9, 10, 36, 50, 51, 83
Continence, 57
Copernican Solar System, 27
Corcoran, Mary Irma, 98
Corporate Unity, 57, 59
Creation, 16, 17, 18, 27, 31, 33, 34, 35, 37, 38, 42, 43, 65, 66, 68, 69, 93, 97, 106

Danielou, Jean, 98
Dante, 19
David, 10, 83
Davies, Horton, 95
Deluge, 59
Descartes, 12
Diekhoff, John S., 36
Divine Grace, 23, 33, 34, 45, 47
Divine Image, 33, 34, 55, 56
Divine Justice, 77, 78, 88
Divine Logos. *See* Logos
Divine Nature, 56, 63, 77, 78, 83

115

Index

Index

Concordia College Library
Bronxville, NY   10708